State of the Nation's Children
Ireland 2010

DECEMBER 2010

OFFICE OF THE MINISTER FOR CHILDREN AND YOUTH AFFAIRS

Office of the Minister for Children and Youth Affairs
Department of Health and Children
Hawkins House
Hawkins Street
Dublin 2
Tel: +353 (0)1 635 4000
Fax: +353 (0)1 674 3223
E-mail: omc@health.gov.ie
Web: www.omcya.ie

Published by Government Publications, Dublin

ISBN 978-1-4064-2321-1

30-01 12/10 (1,000) Brunswick Press Ltd. (24894)

MINISTER'S FOREWORD

As Minister for Children and Youth Affairs, it is my great pleasure to launch the *State of the Nation's Children: Ireland 2010*. This report is the third in a biennial series prepared by the Office of the Minister for Children and Youth Affairs (OMCYA) in association with the Central Statistics Office and the Health Promotion Research Centre at the National University of Ireland, Galway. It fulfils a commitment in the National Children's Strategy to publish key indicators of child well-being on a regular basis.

As with earlier reports in this series, the *State of the Nation's Children: Ireland 2010* presents the most current and most reliable administrative, survey and Census data on the socio-demographic and child well-being indicators that were selected to be part of the National Set of Child Well-Being Indicators back in 2005.

The biennial publication of these reports continues to stimulate impressive improvements in data on child well-being. For the *State of the Nation's Children: Ireland 2010*, new indicators have been developed to close previously identified data gaps and more sophisticated data analyses have been carried out to enable a greater focus on the more vulnerable groups of children in Ireland, including Traveller children, immigrant children and children with a disability and/or chronic illness.

The 2010 edition of this report continues to point to some gaps in the coverage and timeliness of data on child well-being. It is hoped that these can be addressed in the context of the emerging National Data and Research Strategy on Children's Lives, which is being prepared by my Office for publication in 2011.

Barry Andrews, TD
Minister for Children and Youth Affairs
December 2010

Contents

Minister's Foreword iii

Authors viii

Acknowledgements viii

List of Tables ix

List of Figures xvi

Acronyms used xviii

INTRODUCTION

- Outline of report 2
- New developments 3
- Key findings 4

PART 1: SOCIO-DEMOGRAPHICS

- Child population 10
- Child mortality 14
- Family structure 19
- Parental education level 22
- Traveller children 26
- Foreign national children 28
- Children with a disability 32
- Separated children seeking asylum 34

PART 2: CHILDREN'S RELATIONSHIPS

- Relationship with mothers 36
- Relationship with fathers 40
- Talking to parents 44
- Parental involvement in schooling 46
- Eating a main meal together 48
- Friendships 50
- Pets and animals 54
- Bullying 57

PART 3: CHILDREN'S OUTCOMES

EDUCATION OUTCOMES

Enrolment in early childhood care and education 64
Parental satisfaction with early childhood care and education 66
Quality of early childhood care and education 68
School attendance 70
Transfer to second-level education 73
Achievement in reading 75
Achievement in mathematics 78
Achievement in science 81

HEALTH OUTCOMES

Birth weight 86
Breastfeeding 89
Health conditions and hospitalisation 93
Accidents, injuries and hospitalisation 96
Nutritional outcomes 100
Intellectual disability 101
Physical and sensory disability 105
Child welfare and protection: Initial assessment 109
Child welfare and protection: Confirmed abuse 112

SOCIAL, EMOTIONAL AND BEHAVIOURAL OUTCOMES

Participation in decision-making 116
Reading as a leisure activity 120
Smoking cigarettes 122
Alcohol use 126
Cannabis use 130
Sexual health and behaviour 134
Self-esteem 137
Self-reported happiness 140
Youth suicide 143
Physical activity 145
Eating habits 149

PART 4: FORMAL AND INFORMAL SUPPORTS

Public expenditure on education 154
At risk of poverty 158
Consistent poverty 160
Availability of housing for families with children 162
Community characteristics 165
Environment and places 169
Garda Juvenile Diversion Programme referrals 174
Antenatal care 179
Childhood immunisation 182
Accessibility of basic health services 189
Children and young people in care 191
Mental health referrals 195

APPENDICES

Appendix 1: Main data sources, definitions and relevant technical notes 200
Appendix 2: NUTS Classifications 219

INDEX

221

AUTHORS

The main authors of this *State of the Nation's Children: Ireland 2010* report are:

- Anne-Marie Brooks, Office of the Minister for Children and Youth Affairs;
- Sinéad Hanafin, Office of the Minister for Children and Youth Affairs;
- Helen Cahill, Central Statistics Office;
- Saoirse Nic Gabhainn, Health Promotion Research Centre, National University of Ireland, Galway;
- Michal Molcho, Health Promotion Research Centre, National University of Ireland, Galway.

ACKNOWLEDGEMENTS

We would like to thank all the people and organisations who provided data for this 2010 report, especially: Antoinette Daly, Health Research Board (National Psychiatric In-Patient Reporting System); Declan Smyth, Central Statistics Office (Census of the Population); Eithne Tiernan, Central Statistics Office (Childcare Module, Quarterly National Household Survey); Marian McCann and Pamela Lafferty, Central Statistics Office (European Union - Survey on Income and Living Conditions); Maria Crowley and Kieran O'Shea, Central Statistics Office (Vital Statistics); Sarah Craig, Health Research Board (National Intellectual Disability Database and National Physical and Sensory Disability Database); David Millar, Education Research Centre (National Educational Welfare Board Database); Patricia Heavey, National Nutrition Surveillance Centre (European Childhood Obesity Surveillance Initiative); Rachel Perkins and Gerry Shiel, Education Research Centre (Programme for International Student Assessment); Nicola Tickner, Tom Healy and Gillian Golden, Department of Education and Skills (Education Statistics); Gráinne Cosgrove, Department of Health and Children (Hospital In-Patient Enquiry System); Jason Sibley and Anna Lloyd, National Treatment Purchase Fund (Patient Treatment Register); John Nolan and Joseph Murphy, Health Service Executive (Childcare Interim Dataset); Colette Kelly and Amanda Fitzgerald, Health Promotion Research Centre, National University of Ireland, Galway (Health Behaviour of School-aged Children (HBSC) Survey); Maresa Duignan, Office of the Minister for Children and Youth Affairs (ECCE database); Aisling Mulligan and Sheelagh Bonham, Economic and Social Research Institute (National Perinatal Reporting System); and Sarah Gee, Health Protection Surveillance Centre (Immunisation Uptake Statistics).

We are also very grateful to all the people who provided feedback on individual indicators and the children, families and others who provide the data included in this report.

LIST OF TABLES

Table 1: Number of children under 18, by age and gender (2009) 10
Table 2: Number of children and percentage of population under 18, by gender (selected years 1981-2009) 11
Table 3: Percentage of population under 18 in EU-27, by country (selected years 1988-2008) 12
Table 4: Number and rate (per 10,000) of deaths of children, by age (2005-2009) 14
Table 5: Death rates (per 10,000) of children, by gender (2005-2009) 15
Table 6: Number of deaths of children, by age and main cause of death (2009) 15
Table 7: Infant mortality rate (per 1,000 live births) in EU-27, by country (selected years 1988-2008) 17
Table 8: Rate (per 10,000) of deaths of children across selected countries in EU-27, by age and gender (2007) 18
Table 9: Number and percentage of children under 18 living in a lone-parent household, by population groups (2006) 19
Table 10: Number and percentage of children under 18 living in a lone-parent household, by age and gender (2006) 20
Table 11: Number and percentage of children under 18 living in a lone-parent household, by county (2006) 20
Table 12: Percentage of children under 18, by population groups and educational attainment of mother (2006) 22
Table 13: Percentage of children under 18, by age and educational attainment of mother (2006) 23
Table 14: Number of children under 18, by county and educational attainment of mother (2006) 23
Table 15: Number of Traveller children, by age and gender (2006) 26
Table 16: Number and percentage of Traveller children, by county (2006) 27
Table 17: Number of foreign national children, by age and gender (2006) 28
Table 18: Number and percentage of foreign national children, by county (2006) 30
Table 19: Number and percentage of foreign national children, by nationality (2006) 31
Table 20: Number of children with a disability, by age and gender (2006) 32
Table 21: Number and percentage of children with a disability, by county (2006) 33
Table 22: Number and percentage of separated children seeking asylum, by age and gender (2006-2008) 34
Table 23: Percentage of children who report that they find it easy to talk to their mother when something is really bothering them, by population groups (2006) 36
Table 24: Percentage of children who report that they find it easy to talk to their mother when something is really bothering them, by age, gender and social class (1998, 2002 and 2006) 37

Table 25: Percentage of children who report that they find it easy to talk to their mother when something is really bothering them, by NUTS Region (2006) 38
Table 26: Percentage of children who report that they find it easy to talk to their father when something is really bothering them, by population groups (2006) 40
Table 27: Percentage of children who report that they find it easy to talk to their father when something is really bothering them, by age, gender and social class (1998, 2002 and 2006) 41
Table 28: Percentage of children who report that they find it easy to talk to their father when something is really bothering them, by NUTS Region (2006) 42
Table 29: Percentage of children aged 15 who report that their parents spend time just talking with them several times a week, by population groups (2009) 44
Table 30: Percentage of children aged 15 who report that their parents spend time just talking with them several times a week, by gender and social class (2000, 2006 and 2009) 45
Table 31: Percentage of children aged 15 who report that their parents discuss with them how well they are doing at school several times a week, by population groups (2009) 46
Table 32: Percentage of children aged 15 who report that their parents discuss with them how well they are doing at school several times a week, by gender and social class (2000, 2006 and 2009) 47
Table 33: Percentage of children aged 15 who report that their parents eat a main meal with them around a table several times a week, by population groups (2009) 48
Table 34: Percentage of children aged 15 who report that their parents eat a main meal with them around a table several times a week, by gender and social class (2000, 2006 and 2009) 49
Table 35: Percentage of children who report to have 3 or more friends of the same gender, by population groups (2006) 50
Table 36: Percentage of children who report to have 3 or more friends of the same gender, by age, gender and social class (2002 and 2006) 51
Table 37: Percentage of children who report to have 3 or more friends of the same gender, by NUTS Region (2006) 52
Table 38: Percentage of children who report having a pet of their own or a pet in their family, by population groups (2006) 54
Table 39: Percentage of children who report having a pet of their own or a pet in their family, by age, gender and social class (2006) 55
Table 40: Percentage of children who report having a pet of their own or a pet in their family, by NUTS Region (2006) 56
Table 41: Percentage of children who report having been bullied at school (in the past couple of months), by population groups (2006) 57

Table 42: Percentage of children who report having been bullied at school (in the past couple of months), by age, gender and social class (1998, 2002 and 2006) 58
Table 43: Percentage of children who report having been bullied at school (in the past couple of months), by NUTS Region (2006) 59
Table 44: Percentage of children under 13 years of age who avail of non-parental childcare, by school-going status and household structure (2007) 64
Table 45: Percentage of children under 13 years of age who avail of non-parental childcare, by school-going status and NUTS Region (2007) 65
Table 46: Percentage of households with children under 13 who report they have 'access to high-quality, affordable childcare in the community', by household structure (2007) 66
Table 47: Percentage of households with children under 13 who report they have 'access to high-quality, affordable childcare in the community', by NUTS Region and location (2007) 67
Table 48: Percentage of Early Childhood Care and Education (ECCE) services under contract to deliver the Free Pre-School Year Scheme that meet basic and higher capitation criteria, by City and County Childcare Committees (2010) 68
Table 49: Percentage of children who are absent from school for 20 days or more in the school year, by school-going status (2003/04 - 2007/08) 70
Table 50: Average percentage of children per school who are absent from school for 20 days or more in the school year, by selected school characteristics (2007/08) 71
Table 51: Average percentage of children per school who are absent from school for 20 days or more in the school year, by school type and county (2007/08) 72
Table 52: Number and percentage of children leaving national schools, by destination (2005/06 - 2009/10) 74
Table 53: Mean score for children aged 15 based on the OECD-PISA Reading Literacy Scale, by population groups (2009) 75
Table 54: Mean score for children aged 15 based on the OECD-PISA Reading Literacy Scale, by gender and social class (2003, 2006 and 2009) 76
Table 55: Mean score for children aged 15 based on the OECD-PISA Mathematics Literacy Scale, by population groups (2009) 78
Table 56: Mean score for children aged 15 based on the OECD-PISA Mathematics Literacy Scale, by gender and social class (2003, 2006 and 2009) 79
Table 57: Mean score for children aged 15 based on the OECD-PISA Combined Scientific Literacy Scale, by population groups (2009) 81
Table 58: Mean score for children aged 15 based on the OECD-PISA Combined Scientific Literacy Scale, by gender and social class (2003, 2006 and 2009) 82

Table 59: Percentage of babies born weighing less than 2,500 grams (live and still births), by gender (2004-2008) 86
Table 60: Number and percentage of babies born weighing less than 2,500 grams (live and still births), by mothers' county of residence (2008) 88
Table 61: Percentage of infants who are breastfed (exclusive or combined) on discharge from hospital, by mothers' age (2004-2008) 90
Table 62: Percentage of infants who are breastfed (exclusive or combined) on discharge from hospital, by mothers' county of residence (2008) 92
Table 63: Number and percentage of hospital discharges among children, by age, gender and principal diagnosis (2005-2009) 94
Table 64: Number and percentage of hospital discharges among children, by county of residence (2009) 95
Table 65: Number and percentage of hospital discharges among children with a diagnosis of external causes of injury or poisoning, by age, gender and cause (2005-2009) 97
Table 66: Number and percentage of hospital discharges among children with a diagnosis of external causes of injury or poisoning, by county of residence (2009) 99
Table 67: Percentage of children aged 7 in BMI categories of normal, overweight and obese, by gender (2008) 100
Table 68: Number, percentage and rate (per 10,000) of children under 18 years registered as having an intellectual disability, by age, gender and severity of disability (2005-2009) 102
Table 69: Number and percentage of children under 18 years registered as having an intellectual disability, by HSE Region and Local Health Office Area (2009) 103
Table 70: Number, percentage and rate (per 10,000) of children under 18 years registered as having a physical and/or sensory disability, by age, gender and type of disability (2005-2009) 106
Table 71: Number and percentage of children under 18 years registered as having a physical and/or sensory disability, by HSE Region and Local Health Office Area (2009) 107
Table 72: Number and percentage of child welfare and protection reports that went to initial assessment, by type of concern (2006-2008) 109
Table 73: Number and percentage of child welfare and protection reports that went to initial assessment, by type of concern, HSE Region and Local Health Office Area (2008) 110
Table 74: Number and percentage of confirmed child abuse cases, by type of abuse (2006-2008) 112
Table 75: Number and percentage of confirmed child abuse cases, by type of abuse, HSE Region and Local Health Office Area (2008) 113
Table 76: Percentage of children who report that students at their school participate in making the school rules, by population groups (2006) 116

Table 77: Percentage of children who report that students at their school participate in making the school rules, by age, gender and social class (1998, 2002 and 2006) 117
Table 78: Percentage of children who report that students at their school participate in making the school rules, by NUTS Region (2006) 118
Table 79: Percentage of children aged 15 who report that reading is one of their favourite hobbies, by population groups (2009) 120
Table 80: Percentage of children aged 15 who report that reading is one of their favourite hobbies, by gender and social class (2000, 2006 and 2009) 121
Table 81: Percentage of children who report smoking cigarettes every day, by population groups (2006) 122
Table 82: Percentage of children who report smoking cigarettes every day, by age, gender and social class (1998, 2002 and 2006) 123
Table 83: Percentage of children who report smoking cigarettes every day, by NUTS Region (2006) 124
Table 84: Percentage of children who report to have been drunk at least once in the last 30 days, by population groups (2006) 126
Table 85: Percentage of children who report to have been drunk at least once in the last 30 days, by age, gender and social class (2006) 127
Table 86: Percentage of children who report to have been drunk at least once in the last 30 days, by NUTS Region (2006) 128
Table 87: Percentage of children who report to have taken cannabis at least once in their lifetime, by population groups (2006) 130
Table 88: Percentage of children who report to have taken cannabis at least once in their lifetime, by age, gender and social class (2002 and 2006) 131
Table 89: Percentage of children who report to have taken cannabis at least once in their lifetime, by NUTS Region (2006) 132
Table 90: Number and rate (per 100,000) of births, by mothers' age (2005-2009) 134
Table 91: Number and percentage of births to mothers aged 10-17, by county (2009) 136
Table 92: Percentage of children who report feeling happy with the way they are, by population groups (2006) 137
Table 93: Percentage of children who report feeling happy with the way they are, by age, gender and social class (2006) 138
Table 94: Percentage of children who report feeling happy with the way they are, by NUTS Region (2006) 139
Table 95: Percentage of children who report being happy with their lives at present, by population groups (2006) 140
Table 96: Percentage of children who report being happy with their lives at present, by age, gender and social class (1998, 2002 and 2006) 141
Table 97: Percentage of children who report being happy with their lives at present, by NUTS Region (2006) 142

Table 98: Number and rate (per 100,000) of suicides, by age and gender (2005-2009) 143
Table 99: Suicides as a percentage of total deaths of children aged 10-17, by gender (2005-2009) 144
Table 100: Percentage of children who report being physically active for at least 60 minutes per day on more than 4 days per week, by population groups (2006) 145
Table 101: Percentage of children who report being physically active for at least 60 minutes per day on more than 4 days per week, by age, gender and social class (2002 and 2006) 146
Table 102: Percentage of children who report being physically active for at least 60 minutes per day on more than 4 days per week, by NUTS Region (2006) 147
Table 103: Percentage of children who report to eat breakfast on 5 or more days per week, by population groups (2006) 149
Table 104: Percentage of children who report to eat breakfast on 5 or more days per week, by age, gender and social class (2002 and 2006) 150
Table 105: Percentage of children who report to eat breakfast on 5 or more days per week, by NUTS Region (2006) 151
Table 106: Public expenditure on education as % of GDP in EU-27 (2004-2006) 156
Table 107: Real non-capital public expenditure on education, by educational level (1999-2008) 157
Table 108: Percentage of persons at risk of poverty (2005-2009) 158
Table 109: Percentage of persons experiencing consistent poverty (2005-2009) 160
Table 110: Number and percentage of households with children identified as being in need of social housing, by number of children (selected years 1996-2008) 163
Table 111: Number and percentage of households with children identified as being in need of social housing, by household structure and county (2008) 164
Table 112: Percentage of children who report feeling safe in area where they live, by population groups (2006) 165
Table 113: Percentage of children who report feeling safe in area where they live, by age, gender and social class (2002 and 2006) 166
Table 114: Percentage of children who report feeling safe in area where they live, by NUTS Region (2006) 167
Table 115: Percentage of children who report that there are good places in their area to spend their free time, by population groups (2006) 170
Table 116: Percentage of children who report that there are good places in their area to spend their free time, by age, gender and social class (2002 and 2006) 171
Table 117: Percentage of children who report that there are good places in their area to spend their free time, by NUTS Region (2006) 172
Table 118: Number, percentage and rate (per 10,000) of children aged 10-17 referred/referrals to the Garda Juvenile Diversion Programme, by age, gender and outcome (2005-2009) 175

Table 119: Number and percentage of children aged 10-17 referred/referrals to the Garda Juvenile Diversion Programme, by Region and Division (2009) 177
Table 120: Percentage of mothers attending for antenatal care in the first trimester of pregnancy, by mothers' age (2004-2008) 179
Table 121: Immunisation uptake rates, by age and vaccine type (2005-2009) 183
Table 122: Immunisation uptake rates at 12 months, by HSE Region and Local Health Office Area (2009) 184
Table 123: Immunisation uptake rates at 24 months, by HSE Region and Local Health Office Area (2009) 186
Table 124: Immunisation uptake rates among children of relevant age, by vaccine type and EU-27 (2009) 188
Table 125: Number of children on hospital waiting lists (surgical and medical), by hospital and waiting time (2010) 190
Table 126: Number and percentage of children in the care of the HSE, by age, gender, type of placement and length of stay (2006-2008) 192
Table 127: Number and percentage of children in the care of the HSE, by HSE Region and Local Health Office Area (2008) 193
Table 128: Number, percentage and rate (per 100,000) of admissions to psychiatric hospitals among children, by age, gender and diagnosis (2004-2008) 196
Table 129: Number and percentage of admissions to psychiatric hospitals among children, by county (2008) 197

LIST OF FIGURES

Figure 1: Percentage of population under 18 years in EU-27, by country (2008) 13
Figure 2: Number of deaths of children, by gender and main cause of death (2009) 16
Figure 3: Percentage of children under 18 whose mothers have no formal education or primary education only, by county (2006) 25
Figure 4: Number of foreign national children, by age (2002 and 2006) 29
Figure 5: Percentage of children who report that they find it easy to talk to their mother when something is really bothering them, by country (2006) 39
Figure 6: Percentage of children who report that they find it easy to talk to their father when something is really bothering them, by country (2006) 43
Figure 7: Percentage of children who report to have 3 or more friends of the same gender, by country (2006) 53
Figure 8: Percentage of children who report having been bullied at school (in the past couple of months), by country (2006) 60
Figure 9: Percentage of children leaving national schools and not attending another school, by gender (2005/06 - 2009/10) 74
Figure 10: Mean scores of children aged 15 based on the OECD-PISA Reading Literacy Scale, by OECD country (2009) 77
Figure 11: Mean scores of children aged 15 based on the OECD-PISA Mathematics Literacy Scale, by OECD country (2009) 80
Figure 12: Mean scores of children aged 15 based on the OECD-PISA Combined Scientific Literacy Scale, by OECD country (2009) 83
Figure 13: Percentage of babies born weighing less than 2,500 grams (live and still births), by occupation of mother (2008) 87
Figure 14: Percentage of infants who are breastfed (either exclusive or combined) on discharge from hospital, by mothers' occupation (2008) 91
Figure 15: Number of hospital discharges among children with a diagnosis of external causes of injury or poisoning, by age and gender (2009) 98
Figure 16: Percentage of children who report that students at their school participate in making the school rules, by country (2006) 119
Figure 17: Percentage of children who report smoking cigarettes every day, by country (2006) 125
Figure 18: Percentage of children aged 15 who report to have been drunk at least once in the last 30 days, by country (2006) 129
Figure 19: Percentage of children aged 15 who report to have taken cannabis at least once in their lifetime, by country (2006) 133
Figure 20: Number of births to mothers aged 10-17 (2005-2009) 135

Figure 21: Percentage of children who report being physically active for at least 60 minutes per day on more than 4 days per week, by country (2006) 148
Figure 22: Percentage of children who report to eat breakfast on 5 or more days per week, by country (2006) 152
Figure 23: Public expenditure on education in Ireland and in EU-27 (1998-2007) 155
Figure 24: Percentage of children under 18 at risk of poverty by EU-27 (2008) and percentage of children under 18 at risk of poverty by NUTS Region (2009) 159
Figure 25: Percentage of persons experiencing consistent poverty by household structure (2009) and percentage of children experiencing consistent poverty by NUTS Region (2009) 161
Figure 26: Percentage of children who report feeling safe in the area where they live, by country (2006) 168
Figure 27: Percentage of children who report that there are good places in their area to spend their free time, by country (2006) 173
Figure 28: Percentage referrals to the Garda Juvenile Diversion Programme, by type of offence (2009) 176
Figure 29: Percentage of mothers attending for antenatal care in the first trimester of pregnancy, by mothers' occupation (2008) 180
Figure 30: Percentage of mothers attending for antenatal care in the first trimester of pregnancy, by mothers' county of residence (2008) 181

ACRONYMS USED

BCG	Bacillus Calmette-Guerin vaccine
BMI	Body Mass Index
CPI	Consumer Price Index
CSO	Central Statistics Office
D3	Diphtheria and Tetanus vaccine
DEIS	Delivering Equality of Opportunity in Schools
DTaP3	Diphtheria, Tetanus and Pertussis vaccine
ERC	Education Research Centre
ESPAD	European School Survey Project on Alcohol and Other Drugs
ESRI	Economic and Social Research Institute
EU	European Union
EU-25 average	Average result for 25 EU Member States
EU-27 average	Average result for 27 EU Member States
Eurostat	Statistical Office of the European Communities
EU-SILC	EU Survey on Income and Living Conditions
GCSE	General Certificate of Secondary Education
GDP	Gross Domestic Product
GNP	Gross National Product
GNI	Gross National Income
GRO	General Register's Office
HBSC	Health Behaviour in School-aged Children Survey
HFA-DB	European Health for All Database
HiB3	Haemophilus Influenzae Type B vaccine
HIPE	Hospital In-Patient Enquiry System
HPSC	Health Protection Surveillance Centre
HRB	Health Research Board
HSE	Health Service Executive
ICD-9-CM	Clinical modification of the 9th Revision of the International Classification of Diseases
ICD-10	World Health Organization's International Classification of Diseases category
ICD-10-AM	Australian modification of ICD-10
LAAHN	Local Authority Assessment of Housing Need
MenC3	Meningococcal Type C disease vaccine
MMR	Measles, Mumps and Rubella vaccine
NCVA	National Council for Vocational Awards
NESF	National Economic and Social Forum
NEWB	National Educational Welfare Board

NHS	National Health Service
NIDD	National Intellectual Disability Database
NPIRS	National Psychiatric In-Patient Reporting System
NPRS	National Perinatal Reporting System
NPSDD	National Physical and Sensory Disability Database
NTPF	National Treatment Purchase Fund
NUIG	National University of Ireland, Galway
NUTS	Nomenclature of Territorial Units for Statistics
OECD	Organization for Economic Co-operation and Development
OMCYA	Office of the Minister for Children and Youth Affairs
PHN	Public Health Nurse
Polio3	Poliomyelitis vaccine
PISA	Programme for International Student Assessment Survey
PPSN	Personal Public Service Number
PTR	Patient Treatment Register
P3	Pertussis vaccine
QNHS	Quarterly National Household Survey
T3	Tetanus vaccine
UNESCO	United Nations Educational, Scientific and Cultural Organization
WHO	World Health Organization

INTRODUCTION

This is Ireland's third biennial *State of the Nation's Children* report. These reports, which provide the most up-to-date data on all indicators in the National Set of Child Well-Being Indicators, aim to:

- chart the well-being of children in Ireland;
- track changes over time;
- benchmark progress in Ireland relative to other countries;
- highlight policy issues arising.

OUTLINE OF REPORT

This *State of the Nation's Children* report is presented in four sections, as follows:

- **Part 1: Socio-demographics:** This section provides information on the child population, child mortality, family structure, parental education level, Traveller children, foreign national children, children with a disability and separated children seeking asylum. Data are largely drawn from Vital Statistics, the Census of Population and Population Estimates.
- **Part 2: Children's relationships:** This section provides information on children's relationships with their parents and peers, including, for example, levels of reported bullying and children's friendships. Data are drawn from the Health Behaviour of School-aged Children (HBSC) surveys and the Programme for International Student Assessment (PISA) surveys.
- **Part 3: Children's outcomes:** This section provides information on children's health outcomes, educational outcomes, and social, emotional and behavioural outcomes, including, for example, daily smoking, alcohol and drug use, births to teenage girls, health conditions and hospitalisation, educational attainment and self-reported happiness. Data are drawn from the Health Behaviour of School-aged Children (HBSC) surveys, the Programme for International Student Assessment (PISA) surveys, the National Intellectual Disability Database, the National Physical and Sensory Disability Database, and the National Perinatal Reporting System, among others.
- **Part 4: Formal and informal supports:** This section provides information on a range of supports, both formal and informal, including school, housing, antenatal care, immunisation and economic. Data are drawn from the European Union Survey of Income and Living Conditions (EU-SILC), Health Behaviour of School-aged

Children (HBSC) surveys, National Perinatal Reporting System, Vital Statistics, the Triennial Assessment of Housing Needs and the Programme for International Student Assessment (PISA) surveys, among others.

NEW DEVELOPMENTS

This *State of the Nation's Children: Ireland 2010* represents a significant advance on earlier reports in this series. In this report, new indicators have been introduced, existing indicators have been strengthened through more sophisticated disaggregation and analytical techniques, and critical data gaps have been closed. While it has not been possible to update all indicators in this report, previously published data from the 2006 and 2008 reports have been maximised in such a way that tells us something new about child well-being in Ireland.

New indicators

This report includes a number of new indicators that fill previously identified data gaps around the areas of disability; accidents, injuries and hospitalisation; quality of early childhood care and education; and nutritional outcomes (*see below*). Due to data issues, existing indicators on youth homelessness and screening for growth and development have been excluded from this report.

INDICATOR	MEASURE	DATA SOURCE
Children with a disability	The number of children with a disability.	Census of the Population
Accidents, injuries and hospitalisation	The number of hospital discharges among children with a diagnosis of external causes of injury or poisoning.	Hospital In-Patient Enquiry System
Quality of early childhood care and education	The percentage of households with children under 13 years of age who report they have 'access to high-quality, affordable childcare in the community'.	Childcare Module of the Quarterly National Household Survey
	The percentage of Early Childhood Care and Education (ECCE) services under contract to deliver the Free Pre-School Year Scheme that meet basic and higher capitation criteria.	ECCE Database
Nutritional outcomes	The percentage of children aged 7 in the BMI categories of normal, overweight and obese.	WHO European Childhood Obesity Surveillance Initiative

New disaggregation

In earlier reports, indicators were disaggregated according to age, gender, social class and geographic location. Due to data availability issues, further disaggregation across vulnerable groups of children was not possible. Since the publication of the last report (2008), significant efforts have been made to address this. The Office of the Minister for Children and Youth Affairs (OMCYA) liaised with, and welcomes the cooperation of, a number of data providers who have worked to identify vulnerable groups of children in their data sets. In this report, a particular focus is given to Traveller children, immigrant children and children with a disability and/or chronic illness.

Statistical significance

In earlier reports, differences across age, gender, social class and geographic location were simply described. As part of an ongoing effort to improve these reports and again with the cooperation of data providers, the *State of the Nation's Children: Ireland 2010* includes significance testing to assess if these differences are statistically significant.

KEY FINDINGS

- Ireland continues to have the highest proportion of children in the European Union (Population Estimates, Central Statistics Office, 2009).
- The majority of child deaths occur in the period of infancy (less than one year of age) (Vital Statistics, Central Statistics Office, 2009).
- Approximately one in 6 children in Ireland live in a lone-parent household (Census of the Population, Central Statistics Office, 2006).
- Nearly one-third of foreign national children live in families where their mother has a third-level qualification (Census of the Population, Central Statistics Office, 2006).
- Almost half of the total Traveller population of Ireland are under 18 years of age (Census of the Population, Central Statistics Office, 2006).
- Foreign national children account for approximately 6% of the total child population of Ireland (Census of the Population, Central Statistics Office, 2006).
- Almost two-thirds of children with a disability are boys (Census of the Population, Central Statistics Office, 2006).

- The number of separated children seeking asylum has decreased (Child Care Interim Data Set, Health Service Executive, 2008).
- Older children find it more difficult to talk to their mothers when something is really bothering them (HBSC Survey, Health Promotion Research Centre, 2006).
- The percentage of children who report that they find it easy to talk to their fathers when something is really bothering them has increased from approximately 48% in 1998 to 60% in 2006 (HBSC Survey, Health Promotion Research Centre, 2006).
- Significantly more girls than boys report that their parents spend time just talking with them (PISA Survey, Education Research Centre, 2009).
- There has been a significant decrease in the percentage of 15-year-old children who report that their parents discuss with them how well they are doing at school (PISA Survey, Education Research Centre, 2009).
- There has been a significant decrease in the percentage of 15-year-old children who report that their parents eat a main meal with them around a table (PISA Survey, Education Research Centre, 2009).
- Almost 9 out of 10 children have 3 or more friends of the same gender (HBSC Survey, Health Promotion Research Centre, 2006).
- The percentage of children who report to have a pet of their own or a pet in the family is significantly lower among Traveller children and among immigrant children (HBSC Survey, Health Promotion Research Centre, 2006).
- Immigrant children and children with a disability and/or chronic illness are more likely to report to have been bullied at school (HBSC Survey, Health Promotion Research Centre, 2006).
- Almost one in 3 children under 13 years of age avail of non-parental childcare (Childcare Module, Quarterly National Household Survey, Central Statistics Office, 2007).
- Households in the Mid-West region are most likely to report that they have access to high-quality, affordable childcare in the community (Childcare Module, Quarterly National Household Survey, Central Statistics Office, 2007).
- 82% of Early Childhood Care and Education (ECCE) services under contract to deliver the Free Pre-School Year Scheme meet basic capitation criteria and 11% meet higher capitation criteria (ECCE Database, 2010).

- One in every 8 primary school children and one in every 6 post-primary school children miss 20 days or more in the school year (National Educational Welfare Board, 2007/08).
- The majority of children leaving national schools are known to have either progressed to another form of schooling or have emigrated with their families (Education Statistics, Department of Education and Skills, 2009/10).
- There has been a significant decline in reading literacy scores among 15-year-olds in Ireland (PISA Survey, Education Research Centre, 2009).
- Mathematics literacy scores of 15-year-olds in Ireland are significantly below the OECD average (PISA Survey, Education Research Centre, 2009).
- Science literacy scores of 15-year-olds in Ireland are significantly above the OECD average (PISA Survey, Education Research Centre, 2009).
- The percentage of low birth weight babies has remained relatively stable over the last 5 years (National Perinatal Reporting System, Economic and Social Research Institute, 2008).
- Breastfeeding initiation rates have continued to increase (National Perinatal Reporting System, Economic and Social Research Institute, 2008).
- More than half of the total hospital discharges among children were children under 5 years of age (Hospital In-Patient Enquiry, Department of Health and Children, 2009).
- The numbers of hospital discharges among children with a diagnosis of 'transport accidents', 'intentional self-harm' and 'accidental poisoning' continue to fall (Hospital In-Patient Enquiry, Department of Health and Children, 2009).
- Almost one-quarter of 7-year-old children are either overweight or obese (WHO European Childhood Obesity Surveillance Initiative, National Nutrition Surveillance Centre, 2008).
- Approximately 6 in 10 children registered as having an intellectual disability are boys (National Intellectual Disability Database, Health Research Board, 2009).
- Approximately one in 4 children on the National Physical and Sensory Disability Database are registered as having multiple disabilities (National Physical and Sensory Disability Database, Health Research Board, 2009).

- The number of child welfare and protection reports that went to initial assessment increased by 2,844 over the period 2006-2008 (Child Care Interim Data Set, Health Service Executive, 2008).
- The number of cases of confirmed child abuse has increased (Child Care Interim Data Set, Health Service Executive, 2008).
- The percentage of children who report that students at their school participate in making the school rules has decreased from approximately 33% in 1998 to 23% in 2006 (HBSC Survey, Health Promotion Research Centre, 2006).
- Approximately one-third of 15-year-old children report that reading is one of their favourite hobbies (PISA Survey, Education Research Centre, 2009).
- Daily cigarette smoking is significantly higher among Traveller children (HBSC Survey, Health Promotion Research Centre, 2006).
- Immigrant children are less likely to report to have been drunk at least once in the last 30 days (HBSC Survey, Health Promotion Research Centre, 2006).
- Lifetime cannabis use is significantly higher among boys and Traveller children (HBSC Survey, Health Promotion Research Centre, 2006).
- In 2009, 564 babies were born to teenage girls (Vital Statistics, Central Statistics Office, 2009).
- Approximately 4 in 10 girls aged 15-17 report feeling happy with the way they are (HBSC Survey, Health Promotion Research Centre, 2006).
- Self-reported happiness levels are significantly lower among Traveller children, immigrant children and children with a disability and/or chronic illness (HBSC Survey, Health Promotion Research Centre, 2006).
- In 2009, 21 young children took their own lives (Vital Statistics, Central Statistics Office, 2009).
- Children in Ireland have the highest levels of physical activity among 41 OECD countries (HBSC Survey, Health Promotion Research Centre, 2006).
- Boys and younger children are more likely to eat breakfast on 5 or more days per week (HBSC Survey, Health Promotion Research Centre, 2006).
- Since 2002, Ireland's expenditure on education has increased (Department of Education and Skills, 2007).

- Children in the Midlands region are three times more likely to be at risk of poverty than children in the Dublin region (EU-SILC, Central Statistics Office, 2009).
- The percentage of children in the South-East region experiencing consistent poverty is approximately twice as high as the national average (EU-SILC, Central Statistics Office, 2009).
- The number of households with children in need of social housing has increased by 24% since 2005 (Triennial Assessment of Housing Needs, Department of the Environment, Heritage and Local Government, 2008).
- Traveller children and children with a disability and/or chronic illness are less likely to report feeling safe in the area where they live (HBSC Survey, Health Promotion Research Centre, 2006).
- Traveller children and immigrant children are more likely to report having good places in their area to spend their free time (HBSC Survey, Health Promotion Research Centre, 2006).
- There has been a substantial decrease in the number of children referred to the Garda Juvenile Diversion Programme (An Garda Síochána, 2009).
- Early antenatal care is lowest among younger mothers (National Perinatal Reporting System, Economic and Social Research Institute, 2008).
- In 2009, Roscommon had the highest uptake of the recommended doses of all vaccines among children at 12 and 24 months (Immunisation Uptake Statistics, Health Protection Surveillance Centre, 2009).
- In April 2010, 2,591 children were known to be on a hospital waiting list (Patient Treatment Register, National Treatment Purchase Fund, 2010).
- Almost 9 out of 10 children in the care of the Health Service Executive (HSE) live in foster family homes (Child Care Interim Data Set, Health Service Executive, 2008).
- There has been an increase in the number of children admitted to psychiatric hospitals (National Psychiatric In-Patient Reporting System, Health Research Board, 2008).

PART 1:
SOCIO-DEMOGRAPHICS

CHILD POPULATION

Ireland continues to have the highest proportion of children in the European Union.

Measure

The number of children under 18.

Key findings

- In 2009, there were 1,107,034 children aged under 18 living in Ireland. This accounted for almost one-quarter (24.8%) of the total population of Ireland.

Differences by age, gender and over time

- 567,303 of children under 18 were boys and 539,731 were girls (*see Table 1*).

Table 1: Number of children under 18, by age and gender (2009)

	Boys	Girls	Total	Cumulative Total
Total population (under 18)	**567,303**	**539,731**	**1,107,034**	
Total population (all ages)	**2,217,664**	**2,241,641**	**4,459,305**	
Age				
Under 1	37,758	35,731	73,489	73,489
1	37,040	35,154	72,194	145,683
2	34,800	33,724	68,524	214,207
3	33,116	31,333	64,449	278,656
4	32,569	30,413	62,982	341,638
5	32,332	30,610	62,942	404,580
6	31,927	30,552	62,479	467,059
7	31,519	30,042	61,561	528,620
8	30,967	29,996	60,963	589,583
9	30,814	29,274	60,088	649,671
10	30,678	29,037	59,715	709,386
11	30,423	29,074	59,497	768,883
12	29,529	28,078	57,607	826,490

continued

Table 1 *(continued)*				
Age	**Boys**	**Girls**	**Total**	**Cumulative Total**
13	28,732	27,504	56,236	882,726
14	28,320	26,706	55,026	937,752
15	28,033	26,860	54,893	992,645
16	29,137	27,168	56,305	1,048,950
17	29,609	28,475	58,084	1,107,034

Source: Population Estimates, CSO

- The percentage of children under 18 has decreased over the past 26 years, from 36.2% in 1981 to 24.8% in 2009 (*see Table 2*).
- The number of children under 18 has also decreased over this time period, falling from 1,246,443 in 1981 to 1,013,031 in 2002, but has risen since then to stand at 1,107,034 in 2009.

Table 2: Number of children and percentage of population under 18, by gender (selected years 1981-2009)

Year	Boys	% of all men	Girls	% of all women	Total	% of all ages
1981	638,768	36.9	607,675	35.5	1,246,443	36.2
1986	630,985	35.7	599,165	33.8	1,230,150	34.7
1991	587,655	33.5	557,738	31.5	1,145,393	32.5
1996	550,389	30.6	521,583	28.6	1,071,972	29.6
2002	519,483	26.7	493,548	25.0	1,013,031	25.9
2006	530,973	25.0	505,061	23.8	1,036,034	24.4
2007	541,503	24.9	515,444	23.8	1,056,947	24.4
2008	556,017	25.2	529,241	23.9	1,085,258	24.5
2009	567,303	25.6	539,731	24.1	1,107,034	24.8

Source: Census of the Population and Population Estimates, CSO

Differences by geographic location

- In 2008, Ireland had the highest proportion of children under 18 in the European Union (*see Table 3 and Figure 1*).

Table 3: Percentage of population under 18 in EU-27, by country (selected years 1988-2008)

	1988	1998	2008
EU-27	**21.6**	**20.3**	**19.2**
Country			
Austria	21.2	20.0	19.0
Belgium	21.4	20.9	20.6
Bulgaria	20.9	18.6	16.9
Cyprus	28.8	25.5	21.7
Czech Republic	21.6	19.5	17.9
Denmark	21.2	22.1	22.2
Estonia	23.9	21.3	18.8
Finland	22.5	21.4	20.7
France	23.4	22.9	22.3
Germany	19.4	18.5	17.0
Greece	20.4	18.0	17.4
Hungary	21.6	19.9	18.7
Ireland	**28.4**	**25.6**	**24.5**
Italy	17.7	17.2	17.0
Latvia	23.6	20.8	18.0
Lithuania	25.3	23.2	20.0
Luxembourg	22.1	22.2	21.7
Malta	25.9	23.0	20.3
Netherlands	22.0	22.2	21.6
Poland	26.3	22.7	19.6
Portugal	21.1	19.3	18.6
Romania	24.0	21.8	18.9
Slovakia	26.1	22.9	20.0
Slovenia	21.4	18.8	17.2
Spain	19.7	17.8	17.6
Sweden	22.1	21.7	21.0
United Kingdom	23.1	22.3	21.4

Source: Eurostat

Figure 1: Percentage of population under 18 years in EU-27, by country (2008)

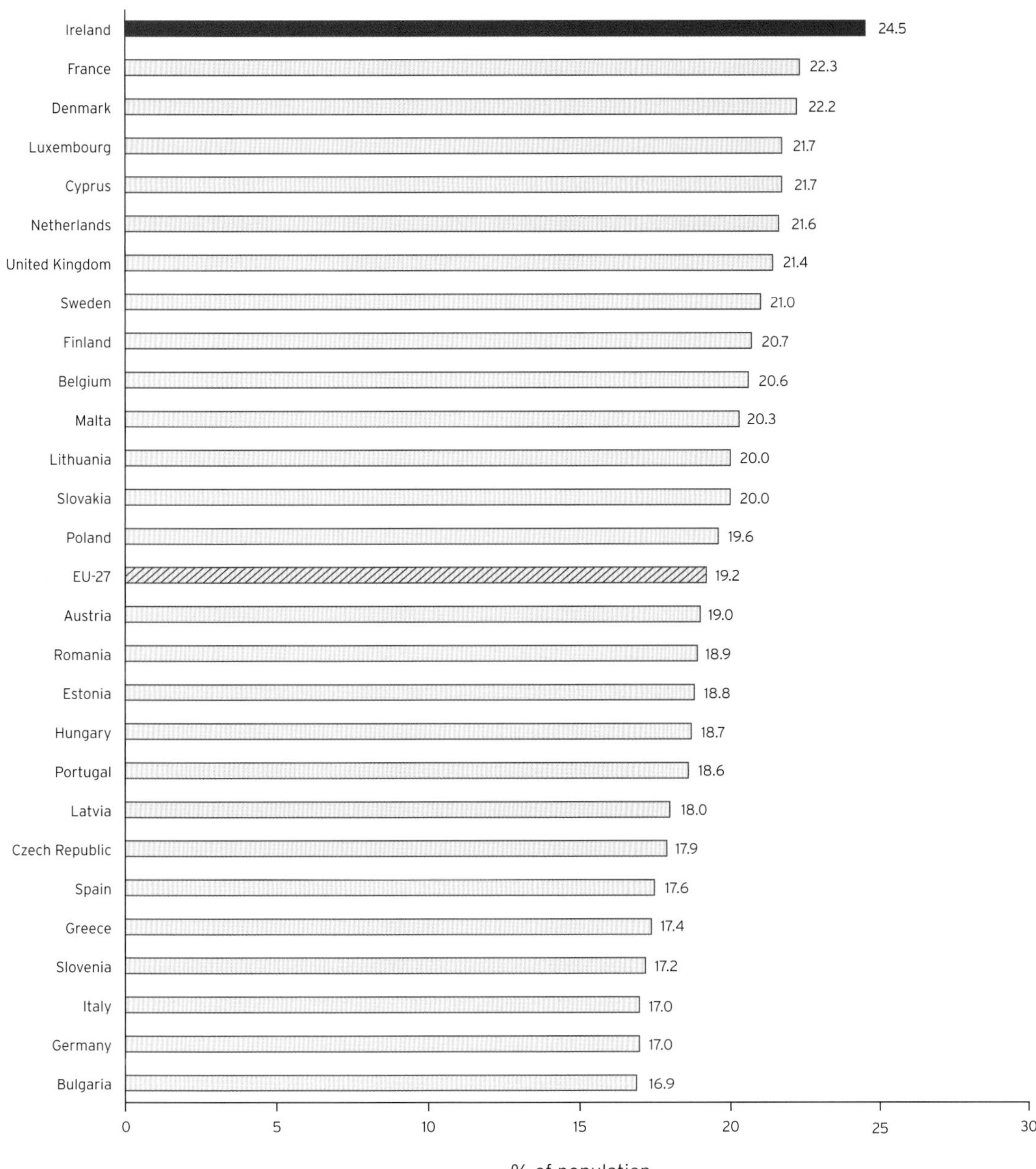

Source: Eurostat

CHILD MORTALITY

The majority of child deaths occur in the period of infancy (less than one year of age).

Measure

The number of deaths of children under 18.

Key findings

- In 2009, there were 419 deaths of children under 18.

Differences by age, gender and over time

- The majority of child deaths occur in the period of infancy (less than 1 year) (*see Table 4*). Infant deaths accounted for 240 of the total of 419 of deaths of children in 2009. This represented a death rate of 32.7 per 10,000 children aged under 1 year, compared to an overall rate of 3.8 per 10,000 children under 18. Apart from the period of infancy, the next highest death rates occurred in the age groups 15-17 and 1-4.

Table 4: Number and rate (per 10,000) of deaths of children, by age (2005-2009)

	2005		2006		2007		2008		2009	
	No.	Rate	No.	Rate	No.	Rate	No.	Rate	No.	Rate
Total	**417**	**4.1**	**421**	**4.1**	**413**	**3.9**	**463**	**4.3**	**419**	**3.8**
Age										
Under 1	236	38.7	255	41.8	230	35.1	290	40.3	240	32.7
1-4	52	2.2	38	1.6	54	2.2	44	1.7	66	2.5
5-9	26	0.9	32	1.1	17	0.6	28	0.9	22	0.7
10-14	38	1.4	35	1.3	50	1.8	46	1.6	33	1.1
15-17	65	3.8	61	3.6	62	3.6	55	3.2	58	3.4

Source: Vital Statistics, CSO

- The death rates were consistently higher for boys than for girls (*see Table 5*). In 2009, the death rate for boys was 4.4 per 10,000 compared to the death rate for girls of 3.2 per 10,000.

- There has been a decrease in infant mortality rates over the past 5 years. In 2005, this rate was 38.7 per 10,000; by 2009, it was 32.7 per 10,000. The death rate of children under 18 has fallen over time, from 4.1 deaths per 10,000 in 2005 to 3.8 deaths per 10,000 in 2009.

Table 5: Death rates (per 10,000) of children, by gender (2005-2009)

	2005	2006	2007	2008	2009
Total	**4.1**	**4.1**	**3.9**	**4.3**	**3.8**
Gender					
Boys	4.2	4.8	4.4	5.1	4.4
Girls	4.0	3.3	3.4	3.4	3.2

Source: Vital Statistics, CSO

Differences by cause of death

- The largest single cause of child deaths was deaths attributable to congenital malformations (*see Table 6*). This was followed by 'certain conditions in the perinatal period' and 'injury and poisoning'.

Table 6: Number of deaths of children, by age and main cause of death (2009)

	Under 1	1-4	5-9	10-14	15-17	All children
	No.	No.	No.	No.	No.	No.
Total	**240**	**66**	**22**	**33**	**58**	**419**
Main cause						
Malignant neoplasms	2	11	6	2	1	22
Certain conditions in the perinatal period	96	1	0	1	0	98
Congenital malformations	104	12	4	3	3	126
Sudden Infant Death Syndrome	22	0	0	0	0	22
Injury and poisoning	1	18	4	21	41	85
Other	15	24	8	6	13	66

Source: Vital Statistics, CSO

- More boys than girls died in each category according to cause of death (*see Figure 2*). This was particularly notable in the category 'injury and poisoning', where more than twice as many deaths were recorded for boys than for girls (59 compared with 26).

Figure 2: Number of deaths of children, by gender and main cause of death (2009)

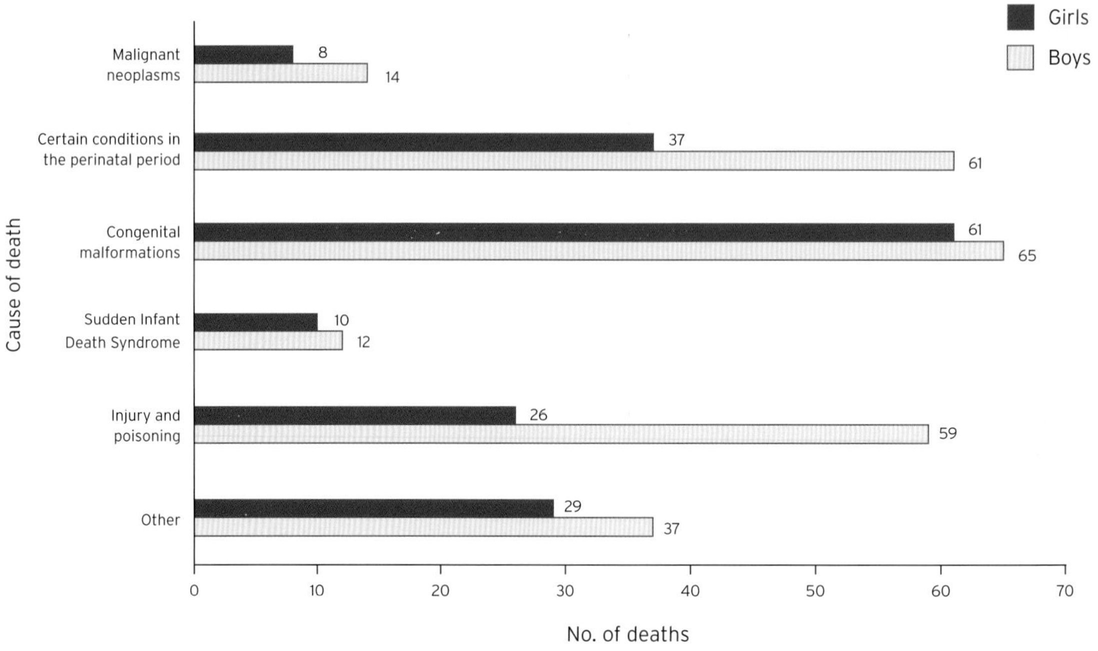

Girls
Boys

Cause of death
Malignant neoplasms 8 14
Certain conditions in the perinatal period 37 61
Congenital malformations 61 65
Sudden Infant Death Syndrome 10 12
Injury and poisoning 26 59
Other 29 37

0 10 20 30 40 50 60 70
No. of deaths

Source: Vital Statistics, CSO

Differences by geographic location

- In 2008, Romania had the highest infant mortality rate (11 per 1,000) and Luxembourg had the lowest infant mortality rate (1.8 per 1,000) (*see Table 7*). The infant mortality rate in Ireland was 3.1 per 1,000.

Table 7: Infant mortality rate (per 1,000 live births) in EU-27, by country (selected years 1988-2008)*

	1988	1998	2008
EU-27	**11.1**	**6.5**	***n/a***
Country			
Austria	8.1	4.9	3.7
Belgium	9.0	5.2	3.4
Bulgaria	13.6	14.4	8.6
Cyprus	13.0	7.0	5.3
Czech Republic	11.0	5.2	2.8
Denmark	7.6	4.7	4.0
Estonia	12.5	9.4	5.0
Finland	6.1	4.2	2.6
France	*n/a*	4.8	3.8
Germany	7.6	4.7	3.5
Greece	11.0	6.7	3.5
Hungary	15.8	9.7	5.6
Ireland	**8.9**	**5.9**	**3.1**
Italy	9.3	5.5	3.7
Latvia	11.0	15.0	6.7
Lithuania	11.6	9.3	4.9
Luxembourg	8.7	5.0	1.8
Malta	8.0	5.1	9.9
Netherlands	6.8	5.2	3.8
Poland	19.9	9.5	5.6
Portugal	13.1	6.0	3.3
Romania	25.4	20.5	11.0
Slovakia	13.3	8.7	5.9
Slovenia	10.0	5.2	2.1
Spain	8.0	4.9	3.5
Sweden	5.8	3.5	2.5
United Kingdom	9.0	5.7	4.7

n/a = not available
* 2007 data used for Ireland for 2008.
Source: Eurostat

- In general, the mortality rate per 10,000 children across the EU-27 is higher for boys than for girls (*see Table 8*).
- Mortality rates are also substantially higher in the 0-4 year age group than for any other age group. The data show that in 2007 Romania had the highest mortality rate for boys in the 0-4 age group (32 per 10,000) and Sweden had the lowest mortality rate (6.7 per 10,000).

Table 8: Rate (per 10,000) of deaths of children across selected countries in EU-27, by age and gender (2007)

	0-4 years		5-9 years		10-14 years		15-19 years	
	Boys	**Girls**	**Boys**	**Girls**	**Boys**	**Girls**	**Boys**	**Girls**
EU-27	**12.3**	**10.0**	**1.2**	**1.0**	**1.5**	**1.2**	**5.2**	**2.2**
Country								
Austria	9.2	7.5	1.0	0.6	1.2	0.9	6.5	2.4
Belgium	11.6	8.5	1.0	0.8	1.5	1.2	5.2	2.4
Bulgaria	26.3	21.9	2.7	2.2	2.8	2.5	7.4	3.4
Cyprus	8.4	9.0	2.7	2.3	1.5	2.7	5.2	2.5
Czech Republic	10.5	7.3	1.1	0.9	1.7	1.0	5.4	2.3
Denmark	10.8	8.1	0.9	0.7	1.2	0.9	4.9	2.2
Estonia	15.3	12.9	2.2	1.4	2.5	2.4	8.0	2.2
Finland	8.1	6.2	0.9	1.1	1.3	1.2	6.5	2.8
France	10.7	8.1	0.9	0.9	1.2	0.9	4.7	1.9
Germany	10.1	8.1	1.1	0.7	1.1	0.9	4.1	1.8
Greece	9.6	8.0	1.4	1.0	1.3	0.9	6.1	1.8
Hungary	14.9	13.4	1.3	1.3	2.2	1.6	5.5	2.2
Ireland	**9.6**	**8.2**	**1.0**	**0.6**	**1.6**	**1.6**	**6.5**	**3.0**
Italy	8.9	7.8	1.1	0.8	1.4	1.0	5.0	2.1
Latvia	22.3	22.6	3.5	1.9	3.6	2.6	9.7	3.7
Lithuania	15.5	14.8	2.8	2.0	3.6	2.8	12.6	3.5
Luxembourg	9.0	4.5	0.0	0.7	0.0	3.4	4.2	2.9
Malta	9.9	16.6	0.9	0.9	2.2	1.6	4.8	0.7
Netherlands	10.5	7.7	0.9	0.9	1.1	1.2	3.4	1.7
Poland	16.5	13.5	1.5	1.1	2.2	1.5	7.1	2.5
Portugal	8.3	7.7	1.4	0.9	1.5	1.7	5.2	2.0
Romania	32.0	25.2	3.4	2.5	3.6	2.3	7.5	3.8
Slovakia	16.9	14.1	2.1	2.2	2.1	1.4	5.7	2.4
Slovenia	7.9	8.1	0.9	1.4	1.0	1.9	5.5	2.9
Spain	10.2	8.9	1.2	1.0	1.6	1.1	5.0	1.8
Sweden	6.7	6.4	0.8	0.9	1.0	0.6	4.4	2.1
United Kingdom	13.3	10.7	1.1	0.8	1.2	1.1	3.9	1.9

Source: Eurostat

FAMILY STRUCTURE

Approximately one in 6 children in Ireland live in a lone-parent household.

Measure

The number of children under 18 living in a lone-parent household.

Key findings

- In 2006, 17.8% (183,744) of children under 18 years of age lived in a lone-parent household.

Differences by population groups

- 24.7% (2,698) of Traveller children, 18.5% (11,631) of foreign national children and 23.1% (9,694) of children with a disability lived in a lone-parent household (*see Table 9*).

Table 9: Number and percentage of children under 18 living in a lone-parent household, by population groups (2006)

	No.	% of all children
All children	**183,744**	**17.8**
Population groups		
Traveller children	2,698	24.7
Foreign national children	11,631	18.5
Children with a disability	9,694	23.1

Source: Census of the Population, CSO

Differences by age and gender

- Almost one in 5 (18.5%) of children aged 15-17 lived in a lone-parent household (*see Table 10*).
- The percentage of boys and girls living in a lone-parent household was broadly similar.

Table 10: Number and percentage of children under 18 living in a lone-parent household, by age and gender (2006)						
	Boys		Girls		Total	
	No.	% of all boys	No.	% of all girls	No.	% of all children
All children	**94,120**	**17.8**	**89,624**	**17.8**	**183,744**	**17.8**
Age						
0-4	25,902	16.8	24,750	16.8	50,652	16.8
5-9	26,884	18.2	25,526	18.2	52,410	18.2
10-14	25,177	17.9	23,773	17.8	48,950	17.9
15-17	16,157	18.4	15,575	18.6	31,732	18.5

Source: Census of the Population, CSO

Differences by geographic location

- Dublin had the highest proportion of children living in a lone-parent household (*see Table 11*).

Table 11: Number and percentage of children under 18 living in a lone-parent household, by county (2006)			
	No.	% within county	% within State
State	**183,744**	**17.8**	**100.0**
County			
Carlow	2,248	17.7	1.2
Cavan	1,988	11.6	1.1
Clare	3,933	13.8	2.1
Cork	18,639	16.1	10.1
Donegal	6,858	17.1	3.7
Dublin	61,903	23.9	33.7
Galway	7,909	14.4	4.3
Kerry	5,076	15.5	2.8
Kildare	7,830	15.5	4.3
Kilkenny	3,077	13.6	1.7
Laois	2,453	13.6	1.3
Leitrim	810	11.4	0.4
Limerick	8,188	19.0	4.5

continued

Table 11 *(continued)*

County	No.	% within county	% within State
Longford	1,664	18.6	0.9
Louth	5,915	20.3	3.2
Mayo	3,902	12.6	2.1
Meath	5,403	12.1	2.9
Monaghan	1,885	13.1	1.0
Offaly	2,892	15.2	1.6
Roscommon	1,679	11.6	0.9
Sligo	2,157	14.9	1.2
Tipperary	6,263	16.5	3.4
Waterford	5,378	20.1	2.9
Westmeath	3,477	16.7	1.9
Wexford	6,332	18.2	3.4
Wicklow	5,885	18.2	3.2

Source: Census of the Population, CSO

PARENTAL EDUCATION LEVEL

Nearly one-third of foreign national children live in families where their mother has a third-level qualification.

Measure

The percentage of children under 18 whose mothers have attained (a) primary, (b) lower secondary, (c) upper secondary or (d) third-level education.

Key findings

- In 2006, 30.6% of children lived in families where the mother had a third-level degree or higher educational attainment; 52.8% of children lived in families where the highest level of educational attainment by mothers was a lower secondary or upper secondary education, while just 6.3% of children lived in families where the mother had either no formal education or primary education only.

Differences by population groups

- Approximately 6 out of every 10 Traveller children (58.9%) lived in families where the mother had either no formal education or primary education only, while 30.7% of foreign national children lived in families where the mother had a third-level degree or higher educational attainment (*see Table 12*).

Table 12: Percentage of children under 18, by population groups and educational attainment of mother (2006)

Highest level of education attained	All children	Traveller children	Foreign national children	Children with a disability
Primary (including no formal education)	6.3	58.9	5.3	9.3
Lower secondary	20.8	11.4	14.9	24.6
Upper secondary	32.0	2.2	25.2	29.3
Third-level (Degree or higher)	30.6	0.9	30.7	26.8
Not stated/not available	10.3	26.7	23.9	10.0

Source: Census of the Population, CSO

Differences by age

- The percentage of children living in families where the mother had a third-level degree or higher educational attainment varied from 38.7% for households with children aged 0-4 to 22.8% for households with children aged 15-17 (*see Table 13*).

Table 13: Percentage of children under 18, by age and educational attainment of mother (2006)

Highest level of education attained	0-4	5-9	10-14	15-17	All children
Primary (including no formal education)	3.7	5.0	7.6	10.9	6.3
Lower secondary	14.6	20.1	24.5	27.2	20.8
Upper secondary	31.0	33.4	32.7	30.3	32.0
Third-level (Degree or higher)	38.7	31.2	26.0	22.8	30.6
Not stated/not available	12.1	10.3	9.2	8.8	10.3

Source: Census of the Population, CSO

Differences by geographic location

- Donegal had the highest proportion of children living in families where the mother had either no formal education or primary education only (*see Table 14 and Figure 3*).

Table 14: Number of children under 18, by county and educational attainment of mother (2006)

	Primary (including no formal education)	Lower secondary	Upper secondary	Third-level (Degree or higher)	Not stated/ not available	Total
State	**63,463**	**209,775**	**322,356**	**308,501**	**103,769**	**1,007,864**
County						
Carlow	785	2,739	3,899	3,414	1,496	12,333
Cavan	999	3,711	5,679	4,873	1,508	16,770
Clare	1,271	4,925	9,558	9,356	2,733	27,843
Cork	5,151	23,002	38,083	37,445	9,961	113,642
Donegal	4,038	10,438	11,082	10,644	3,317	39,519
Dublin	18,723	51,513	70,289	77,319	33,608	251,452
Galway	2,847	8,727	17,814	18,793	5,617	53,798
Kerry	1,748	6,825	10,511	9,970	3,071	32,125
Kildare	2,462	9,362	16,534	16,022	4,962	49,342

continued

Table 14 ***(continued)***

County	Primary (including no formal education)	Lower secondary	Upper secondary	Third-level (Degree or higher)	Not stated/ not available	Total
Kilkenny	1,071	4,487	7,759	7,190	1,603	22,110
Laois	1,027	3,653	6,419	4,776	1,825	17,700
Leitrim	318	1,383	2,592	2,223	486	7,002
Limerick	3,273	9,235	13,227	12,522	3,889	42,146
Longford	743	1,693	2,999	2,299	1,025	8,759
Louth	2,447	6,997	7,990	7,917	3,242	28,593
Mayo	1,816	5,937	11,693	8,596	2,369	30,411
Meath	1,979	8,964	15,024	14,079	3,828	43,874
Monaghan	813	3,549	4,616	3,985	1,178	14,141
Offaly	1,393	4,407	6,351	4,655	1,777	18,583
Roscommon	626	2,642	5,602	4,359	1,068	14,297
Sligo	723	2,465	4,781	5,007	1,234	14,210
Tipperary	2,156	8,150	13,232	10,185	3,404	37,127
Waterford	1,506	5,711	8,480	7,684	2,657	26,038
Westmeath	1,355	4,271	6,646	5,743	2,312	20,327
Wexford	2,498	8,692	11,683	8,606	2,545	34,024
Wicklow	1,695	6,297	9,813	10,839	3,054	31,698

Source: Census of the Population, CSO

Figure 3: Percentage of children under 18 whose mothers have no formal education or primary education only, by county (2006)

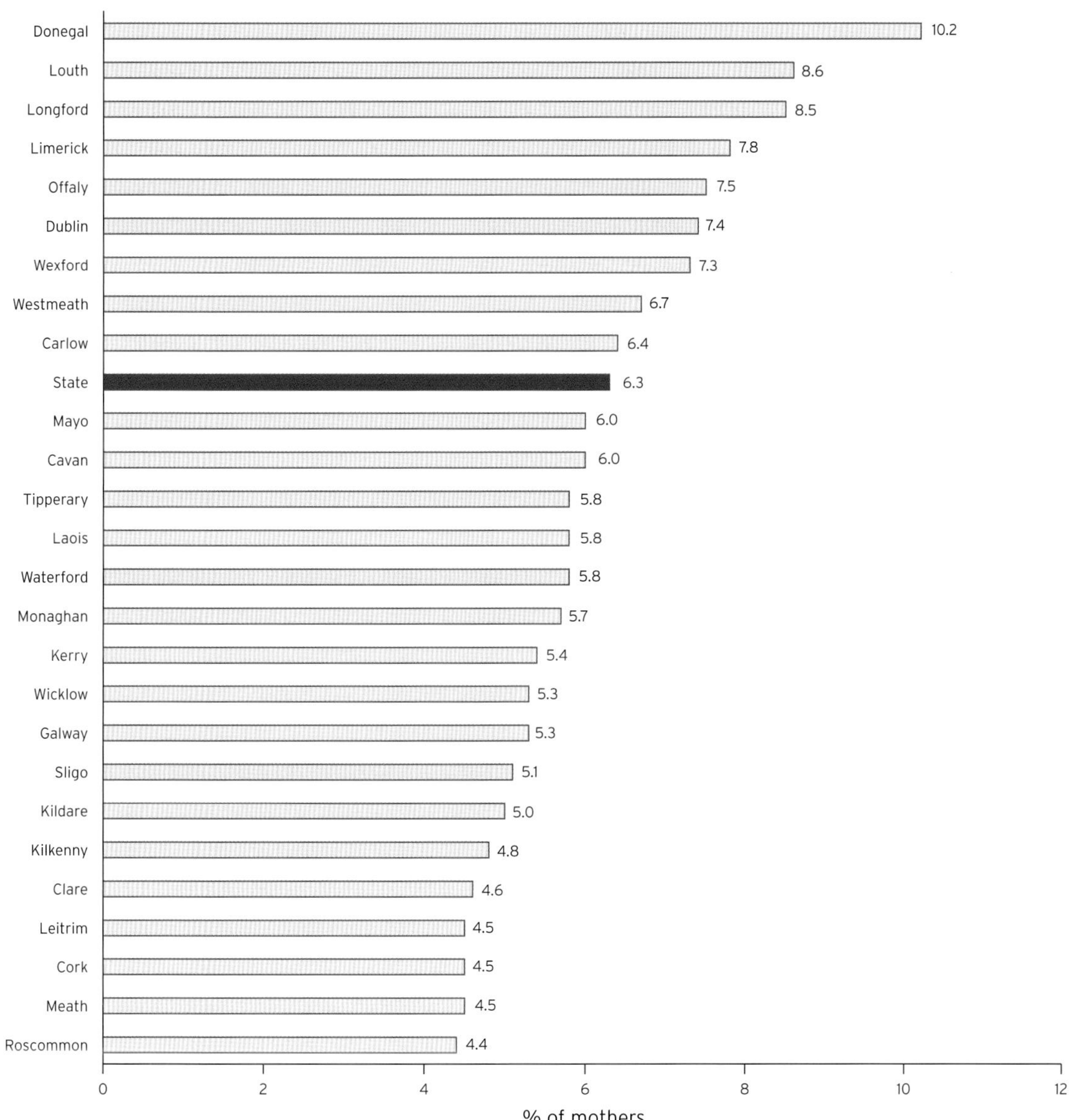

Source: Census of the Population, CSO

TRAVELLER CHILDREN

Almost half of the total Traveller population of Ireland are under 18 years of age.

Measure

The number of Traveller children.

Key findings

- In 2006, there were 10,929 Traveller children in Ireland. This accounted for 1.1% of the total child population of Ireland.

Differences by age and gender

- The number of Traveller boys (5,543) and girls (5,386) was broadly similar (*see Table 15*).

Table 15: Number of Traveller children, by age and gender (2006)

	Boys	Girls	Total
Total (Traveller children)	**5,543**	**5,386**	**10,929**
Total (Traveller population)	**11,028**	**11,407**	**22,435**
Age			
0-4	1,697	1,615	3,312
5-9	1,551	1,478	3,029
10-14	1,504	1,456	2,960
15-17	791	837	1,628

Source: Census of the Population, CSO

Differences by geographic location

- Longford had the highest proportion of Traveller children (*see Table 16*).

Table 16: Number and percentage of Traveller children, by county (2006)

	No. of Traveller children	No. of children	Traveller children as % of all children
State	**10,929**	**1,036,034**	**1.1**
County			
Carlow	119	12,668	0.9
Cavan	93	17,127	0.5
Clare	351	28,565	1.2
Cork	628	116,241	0.5
Donegal	171	40,288	0.4
Dublin	2,532	261,101	1.0
Galway	1,572	55,306	2.8
Kerry	285	33,036	0.9
Kildare	234	50,337	0.5
Kilkenny	200	22,882	0.9
Laois	248	18,013	1.4
Leitrim	99	7,133	1.4
Limerick	631	43,507	1.5
Longford	283	8,930	3.2
Louth	177	29,233	0.6
Mayo	504	30,969	1.6
Meath	354	44,621	0.8
Monaghan	86	14,455	0.6
Offaly	330	19,169	1.7
Roscommon	156	14,503	1.1
Sligo	180	14,610	1.2
Tipperary	462	37,931	1.2
Waterford	205	27,009	0.8
Westmeath	299	21,124	1.4
Wexford	507	34,851	1.5
Wicklow	223	32,425	0.7

Source: Census of the Population, CSO

FOREIGN NATIONAL CHILDREN

Foreign national children account for approximately 6% of the total child population of Ireland.

Measure

The number of foreign national children.

Key findings

- In 2006, there were 62,800 foreign national children in Ireland. This accounted for 6.1% of the total child population of Ireland.

Differences by age, gender and over time

- The number of foreign national boys (31,835) and girls (30,965) was broadly similar (*see Table 17*).

Table 17: Number of foreign national children, by age and gender (2006)

	Boys	Girls	Total
Total	**31,835**	**30,965**	**62,800**
Age			
0-4	6,726	6,570	13,296
5-9	10,341	9,831	20,172
10-14	9,607	9,425	19,032
15-17	5,161	5,139	10,300

Source: Census of the Population, CSO

- The number of foreign national children increased by 57.6%, from 39,838 in 2002 to 62,800 in 2006 (*see Figure 4*).

Figure 4: Number of foreign national children, by age (2002 and 2006)

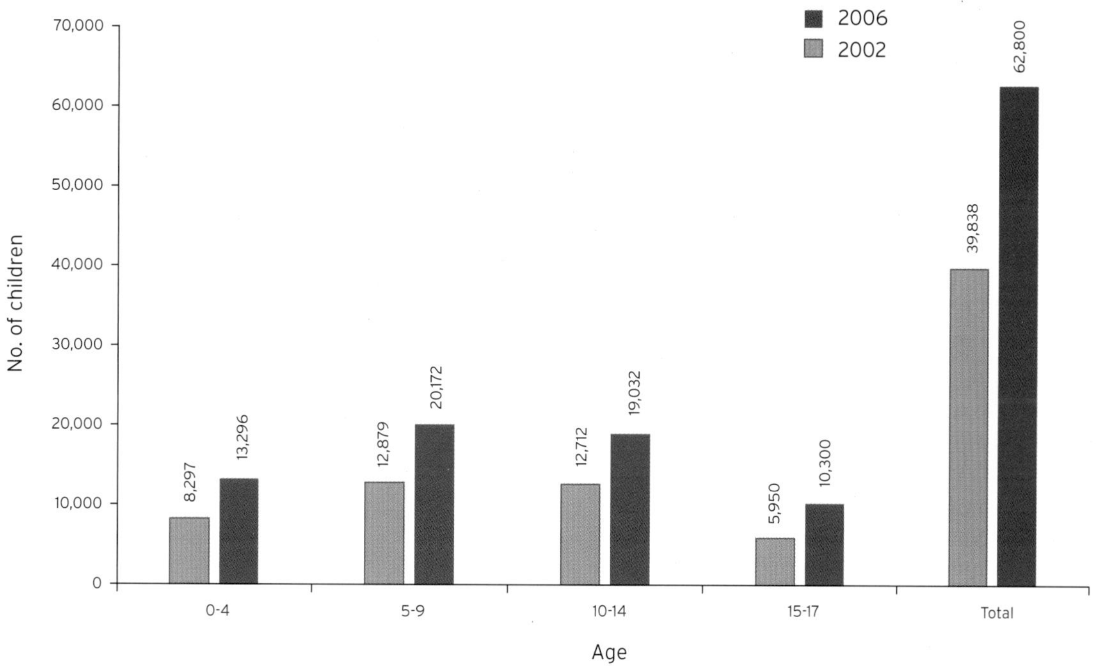

Source: Census of the Population, CSO

Differences by geographic location

- Leitrim had the highest proportion of foreign national children (*see Table 18*).

Table 18: Number and percentage of foreign national children, by county (2006)

	No. of foreign national children	No. of children	Foreign national children as % of all children
State	**62,800**	**1,036,034**	**6.1**
County			
Carlow	752	12,668	5.9
Cavan	1,096	17,127	6.4
Clare	1,858	28,565	6.5
Cork	6,284	116,241	5.4
Donegal	2,195	40,288	5.4
Dublin	17,751	261,101	6.8
Galway	3,763	55,306	6.8
Kerry	2,390	33,036	7.2
Kildare	3,028	50,337	6.0
Kilkenny	996	22,882	4.4
Laois	1,043	18,013	5.8
Leitrim	571	7,133	8.0
Limerick	1,996	43,507	4.6
Longford	638	8,930	7.1
Louth	1,786	29,233	6.1
Mayo	2,083	30,969	6.7
Meath	2,521	44,621	5.6
Monaghan	961	14,455	6.6
Offaly	935	19,169	4.9
Roscommon	1,077	14,503	7.4
Sligo	797	14,610	5.5
Tipperary	2,065	37,931	5.4
Waterford	1,476	27,009	5.5
Westmeath	1,360	21,124	6.4
Wexford	1,744	34,851	5.0
Wicklow	1,634	32,425	5.0

Source: Census of the Population, CSO

- Nearly one-third of foreign national children (31.9%) reported their nationality as British or Northern Irish *(see Table 19)*. Polish was the next most common nationality (8.2% of the total). The only other national minorities with more than 5% of the total number of foreign national children were Nigerians, Americans and Lithuanians.

Table 19: Number and percentage of foreign national children, by nationality (2006)

	No.	%
Total	**62,800**	**100.0**
Nationality		
Australia	677	1.1
France	666	1.1
Germany	1,024	1.6
India	1,232	2.0
Latvia	1,459	2.3
Lithuania	3,179	5.1
Nigeria	4,687	7.5
Other	14,466	23.0
Pakistan	1,101	1.8
Philippines	1,731	2.8
Poland	5,171	8.2
Romania	1,297	2.1
Russia	783	1.2
South Africa	1,186	1.9
United Kingdom	20,010	31.9
USA	4,131	6.6

Source: Census of the Population, CSO

CHILDREN WITH A DISABILITY

Almost two-thirds of children with a disability are boys.

Measure

The number of children with a disability.

Key findings

- In 2006, there were 42,021 children with a disability in Ireland. This accounted for 4.1% of the total child population of Ireland.

Differences by age and gender

- Almost two-thirds (63%) of children with a disability were boys (*see Table 20*).

Table 20: Number of children with a disability, by age and gender (2006)

	Boys	Girls	Total
Total	**26,474**	**15,547**	**42,021**
Age			
0-4	3,122	2,176	5,298
5-9	7,741	4,248	11,989
10-14	10,320	5,649	15,969
15-17	5,291	3,474	8,765

Source: Census of the Population, CSO

Differences by geographic location

- Wicklow had the highest proportion of children with a disability (*see Table 21*).

Table 21: Number and percentage of children with a disability, by county (2006)			
	No. of children with a disability	No. of children	Children with a disability as % of all children
State	**42,021**	**1,036,034**	**4.1**
County			
Carlow	552	12,668	4.4
Cavan	561	17,127	3.3
Clare	1,179	28,565	4.1
Cork	4,605	116,241	4.0
Donegal	1,622	40,288	4.0
Dublin	11,309	261,101	4.3
Galway	1,919	55,306	3.5
Kerry	1,359	33,036	4.1
Kildare	2,123	50,337	4.2
Kilkenny	923	22,882	4.0
Laois	770	18,013	4.3
Leitrim	243	7,133	3.4
Limerick	1,902	43,507	4.4
Longford	342	8,930	3.8
Louth	1,068	29,233	3.7
Mayo	1,024	30,969	3.3
Meath	1,718	44,621	3.9
Monaghan	484	14,455	3.3
Offaly	678	19,169	3.5
Roscommon	463	14,503	3.2
Sligo	641	14,610	4.4
Tipperary	1,682	37,931	4.4
Waterford	973	27,009	3.6
Westmeath	859	21,124	4.1
Wexford	1,503	34,851	4.3
Wicklow	1,519	32,425	4.7

Source: Census of the Population, CSO

SEPARATED CHILDREN SEEKING ASYLUM

The number of separated children seeking asylum has decreased.

Measure

The number of separated children seeking asylum.

Key findings

- In 2008, there were 354 separated children seeking asylum.

Differences by age, gender and over time

- Almost half (47.2%) of the separated children seeking asylum were aged 15-17 years and more than half (52.0%) were boys *(see Table 22).*
- Over the period 2006-2008, the number of separated children seeking asylum has fallen substantially.

Table 22: Number and percentage of separated children seeking asylum, by age and gender (2006-2008)

	2006	2007	2008	
	No.	No.	No.	%
Total	**564**	**362**	**354**	**100.0**
Age				
0-4	35	23	20	5.6
5-9	131	78	63	17.8
10-14	143	86	104	29.4
15-17	255	175	167	47.2
Gender				
Boys	274	169	184	52.0
Girls	290	193	170	48.0

Source: Child Care Interim Data Set, HSE

PART 2: CHILDREN'S RELATIONSHIPS

covering
Relationships with parents
and
Relationships with peers

RELATIONSHIP WITH MOTHERS

Older children find it more difficult to talk to their mothers when something is really bothering them.

Measure

The percentage of children aged 9-17 who report that they find it easy to talk to their mother when something is really bothering them.

Key findings

- In 2006, 78.0% of children aged 9-17 reported that they find it easy to talk to their mother when something is really bothering them.

Differences by population groups

- When compared to other children, Traveller children were less likely to report that they find it easy to talk to their mother when something is really bothering them (*see Table 23*). This difference was statistically significant.
- There were no significant differences between immigrant and non-immigrant children, and between children with and without a disability and/or chronic illness.

Table 23: Percentage of children who report that they find it easy to talk to their mother when something is really bothering them, by population groups (2006)

	%
All children	**78.0**
Traveller status	
Traveller children	70.6
All other children	78.0
Immigrant status	
Immigrant children	78.6
All other children	77.9
Disability and/or Chronic Illness status	
Children with a disability and/or chronic illness	76.8
All other children	78.2

Source: HBSC Survey, Health Promotion Research Centre

Differences by age, gender, social class and over time

- Statistically significant differences were also observed across age, with a lower percentage of older children reporting that they find it easy to talk to their mother when something is really bothering them (*see Table 24*).
- The percentage of children in each social class category and the percentage of boys and girls who report that they find it easy to talk to their mother when something is really bothering them was broadly similar, with no statistical significant differences.

Table 24: Percentage of children who report that they find it easy to talk to their mother when something is really bothering them, by age, gender and social class (1998, 2002 and 2006)

	1998	2002	2006		
	Total (%)	Total (%)	Boys (%)	Girls (%)	Total (%)
All children	**74.0**	**77.6**	**77.5**	**78.4**	**78.0**
Age					
9	–	–	87.5	87.5	87.5
10-11	81.2	86.7	88.0	88.7	88.4
12-14	76.4	79.6	79.8	82.2	81.0
15-17	65.0	71.1	72.1	69.4	70.8
Social class					
SC 1-2	71.6	76.2	78.6	77.7	78.2
SC 3-4	75.0	78.5	78.3	79.3	78.8
SC 5-6	75.6	80.1	78.6	79.4	79.0

Source: HBSC Survey, Health Promotion Research Centre

Differences by geographic location

- Children in the South-East region were more likely to report that they find it easy to talk to their mother when something is really bothering them (79.2%), while children in the Mid-West region were least likely to report this (75.3%) (*see Table 25*). These differences were not statistically significant.

Table 25: Percentage of children who report that they find it easy to talk to their mother when something is really bothering them, by NUTS Region (2006)

	%
All children	**78.0**
NUTS Region	
Border	78.1
Dublin	78.7
Midlands	77.9
Mid-East	77.7
Mid-West	75.3
South-East	79.2
South-West	78.6
West	76.6

Source: HBSC Survey, Health Promotion Research Centre

International comparisons

- From the 2006 HBSC Survey, using the ages of 11, 13 and 15 only to draw international comparisons, 79.5% of children from Ireland reported that they found it easy to talk to their mother when something was really bothering them (*see Figure 5*). This was significantly lower than the HBSC average of 81.5%.
- Among all 40 countries and regions that used this HBSC item, the lowest percentage for this indicator was found among Belgian (French) children (68.0%) and the highest among Slovenian children (90.1%). Overall, children from Ireland ranked 26th.

Figure 5: Percentage of children who report that they find it easy to talk to their mother when something is really bothering them, by country (2006)

Source: HBSC Survey, Health Promotion Research Centre

RELATIONSHIP WITH FATHERS

The percentage of children who report that they find it easy to talk to their fathers when something is really bothering them has increased from approximately 48% in 1998 to 60% in 2006.

Measure

The percentage of children aged 9-17 who report that they find it easy to talk to their father when something is really bothering them.

Key findings

- In 2006, 59.8% of children aged 9-17 reported that they found it easy to talk to their father when something was really bothering them.

Differences by population groups

- When compared to other children, there were no significant differences in the percentages of Traveller children, immigrant children and children with a disability and/or chronic illness who reported that they find it easy to talk to their father when something is really bothering them (*see Table 26*).

Table 26: Percentage of children who report that they find it easy to talk to their father when something is really bothering them, by population groups (2006)

	%
All children	**59.8**
Traveller status	
Traveller children	55.9
All other children	59.7
Immigrant status	
Immigrant children	61.4
All other children	59.7
Disability and/or Chronic Illness status	
Children with a disability and/or chronic illness	58.8
All other children	59.9

Source: HBSC Survey, Health Promotion Research Centre

Differences by age, gender, social class and over time

- Statistically significant differences across age and gender were observed, with a higher percentage of younger children and a lower percentage of girls reporting that they find it easy to talk to their father when something is really bothering them (*see Table 27*).
- The percentage of children in each social class category who reported that they find it easy to talk to their father when something is really bothering them was broadly similar, with no statistical significant differences.

Table 27: Percentage of children who report that they find it easy to talk to their father when something is really bothering them, by age, gender and social class (1998, 2002 and 2006)

	1998	2002	2006		
	Total (%)	Total (%)	Boys (%)	Girls (%)	Total (%)
All children	**48.1**	**56.2**	**67.1**	**52.1**	**59.8**
Age					
9	–	–	79.3	77.5	78.4
10-11	60.2	71.3	80.0	66.1	72.2
12-14	50.0	57.8	72.0	54.7	63.7
15-17	36.7	47.5	58.5	42.9	51.1
Social class					
SC 1-2	44.1	56.1	68.0	54.4	61.4
SC 3-4	49.2	56.8	68.4	51.6	60.1
SC 5-6	47.9	56.4	66.3	52.8	59.3

Source: HBSC Survey, Health Promotion Research Centre

Differences by geographic location

- Children in the South-East region were more likely to report that they find it easy to talk to their father when something is really bothering them (61.4%), while children in the Mid-West region were least likely to report this (57.3%) (*see Table 28*). These differences were statistically significant.

Table 28: Percentage of children who report that they find it easy to talk to their father when something is really bothering them, by NUTS Region (2006)

	%
All children	**59.8**
NUTS Region	
Border	59.0
Dublin	60.5
Midlands	57.9
Mid-East	58.9
Mid-West	57.3
South-East	61.4
South-West	58.9
West	59.4

Source: HBSC Survey, Health Promotion Research Centre

International comparisons

- From the 2006 HBSC Survey, using the ages of 11, 13 and 15 only to draw international comparisons, 62.9% of children from Ireland reported that they found it easy to talk to their father when something was really bothering them (*see Figure 6*). This was slightly higher than the HBSC average of 61.7%, but not statistically significant.
- Among all 40 countries and regions that used this HBSC item, the lowest percentage for this indicator was found among children from the USA (46.8%) and highest among children from Slovenia (77.2%). Overall, children from Ireland ranked 18th.

Figure 6: Percentage of children who report that they find it easy to talk to their father when something is really bothering them, by country (2006)

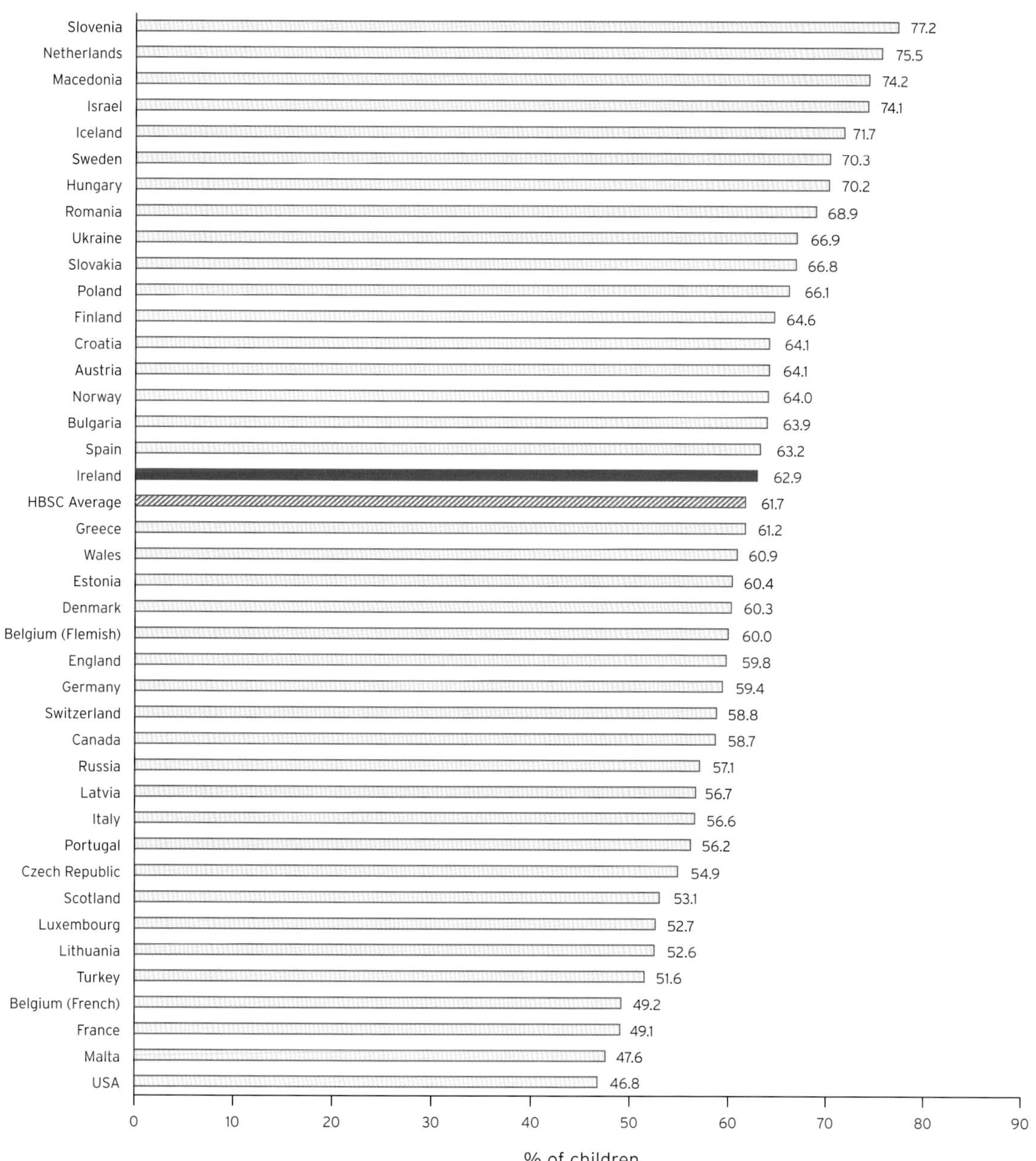

Source: HBSC Survey, Health Promotion Research Centre

TALKING TO PARENTS

Significantly more girls than boys report that their parents spend time just talking with them.

Measure

The percentage of children aged 15 who report that their parents spend time just talking with them several times a week.

Key findings

- In 2009, 59.8% of children aged 15 reported that their parents spend time just talking with them several times a week.

Differences by population groups

- The percentages of Traveller children and immigrant children who reported that their parents spend time just talking with them several times a week did not differ significantly from the corresponding percentages of non-Traveller and non-immigrant children (*see Table 29*).

Table 29: Percentage of children aged 15 who report that their parents spend time just talking with them several times a week, by population groups (2009)

	%
All children	**59.8**
Traveller status	
Traveller children	49.0
All other children	60.0
Immigrant status	
Immigrant children	51.9
All other children	60.4

Source: PISA Survey, Education Research Centre

Differences by gender, social class and over time

- The percentage of girls (70.8%) who reported that their parents spend time just talking with them several times a week was significantly higher than the corresponding percentage of boys (48.9%) *(see Table 30)*.
- Children from the highest social class category (63.0%) were significantly more likely to report that their parents spend time just talking with them several times a week when compared to children from the lowest social class category (57.1%).
- In 2009, the percentage of children (59.8%) who reported that their parents spend time just talking with them several times a week was significantly lower than the corresponding percentage in 2006 (64.7%) and 2000 (61.6%).

Table 30: Percentage of children aged 15 who report that their parents spend time just talking with them several times a week, by gender and social class (2000, 2006 and 2009)

	2000	2006	2009
All children	**61.6**	**64.7**	**59.8**
Gender			
Boys	52.8	55.6	48.9
Girls	70.3	73.4	70.8
Social class			
High SES	62.3	66.6	63.0
Medium SES	61.9	64.6	60.2
Low SES	60.4	63.0	57.1

Source: PISA Survey, Education Research Centre

PARENTAL INVOLVEMENT IN SCHOOLING

There has been a significant decrease in the percentage of 15-year-old children who report that their parents discuss with them how well they are doing at school.

Measure

The percentage of children aged 15 who report that their parents discuss with them how well they are doing at school several times a week.

Key findings

- In 2009, 42.8% of children aged 15 reported that their parents discuss with them how well they are doing at school several times a week.

Differences by population groups

- When compared to other children, immigrant children were less likely to report that their parents discuss with them how well they are doing at school several times a week (*see Table 31*). This difference was statistically significant.
- There was no significant difference between Traveller children and non-Traveller children.

Table 31: Percentage of children aged 15 who report that their parents discuss with them how well they are doing at school several times a week, by population groups (2009)

	%
All children	**42.8**
Traveller status	
Traveller children	54.6
All other children	42.6
Immigrant status	
Immigrant children	30.4
All other children	42.8

Source: PISA Survey, Education Research Centre

Differences by gender, social class and over time

- The percentage of girls (46.3%) who reported that their parents discuss with them how well they are doing at school several times a week was significantly higher than the corresponding percentage of boys (39.4%) (*see Table 32*).
- Children in the lowest social class category (37.9%) were significantly less likely to report that their parents discuss with them how well they are doing at school several times a week when compared to children in the highest and medium social class categories (46.6% and 43.6% respectively).
- In 2009, the percentage of children (42.8%) who reported that their parents discuss with them how well they are doing at school several times a week was significantly lower than the corresponding percentages in 2006 (48.0%) and 2000 (47.9%).

Table 32: Percentage of children aged 15 who report that their parents discuss with them how well they are doing at school several times a week, by gender and social class (2000, 2006 and 2009)

	2000	2006	2009
All children	**47.9**	**48.0**	**42.8**
Gender			
Boys	45.7	44.1	39.4
Girls	50.0	51.6	46.3
Social class			
High SES	51.3	50.0	46.6
Medium SES	46.7	50.0	43.6
Low SES	45.1	43.5	37.9

Source: PISA Survey, Education Research Centre

EATING A MAIN MEAL TOGETHER

There has been a significant decrease in the percentage of 15-year-old children who report that their parents eat a main meal with them around a table.

Measure

The percentage of children aged 15 who report that their parents eat a main meal with them around a table several times a week.

Key findings

- In 2009, 72.4% of children aged 15 reported that their parents eat a main meal with them around a table several times a week.

Differences by population group

- The percentages of Traveller children and immigrant children who reported that their parents eat a main meal with them around a table several times a week did not differ significantly from the corresponding percentages of non-Traveller and non-immigrant children (*see Table 33*).

Table 33: Percentage of children aged 15 who report that their parents eat a main meal with them around a table several times a week, by population groups (2009)

	%
All children	**72.4**
Traveller status	
Traveller children	61.8
All other children	72.6
Immigrant status	
Immigrant children	68.8
All other children	73.2

Source: PISA Survey, Education Research Centre

Differences by gender, social class and over time

- The percentage of girls (74.6%) who reported that their parents eat a main meal with them around a table several times a week did not differ significantly from the corresponding percentage of boys (70.1%) (*see Table 34*).
- Children in the lowest social class category (66.9%) were significantly less likely to report that their parents eat a main meal with them around a table several times a week when compared to children in the highest and medium social class categories (77.1% and 73.6% respectively).
- In 2009, the percentage of children (72.4%) who reported that their parents eat a main meal with them around a table several times a week was significantly lower than the corresponding percentage in 2000 (77.1%).

Table 34: Percentage of children aged 15 who report that their parents eat a main meal with them around a table several times a week, by gender and social class (2000, 2006 and 2009)

	2000	2006	2009
All children	**77.1**	**74.5**	**72.4**
Gender			
Boys	77.6	73.7	70.1
Girls	76.5	75.3	74.6
Social class			
High SES	78.5	78.2	77.1
Medium SES	78.6	75.2	73.6
Low SES	73.5	70.7	66.9

Source: PISA Survey, Education Research Centre

FRIENDSHIPS

Almost 9 out of 10 children have 3 or more friends of the same gender.

Measure

The percentage of children aged 9-17 who report to have 3 or more friends of the same gender.

Key findings

- In 2006, 89.5% of children aged 9-17 reported that they had 3 or more friends of the same gender.

Differences by population groups

- When compared to other children, Traveller children and immigrant children were less likely to report having 3 or more friends of the same gender (*see Table 35*). These differences were statistically significant.
- There were no significant differences between children with and children without a disability and/or chronic illness.

Table 35: Percentage of children who report to have 3 or more friends of the same gender, by population groups (2006)

	%
All children	**89.5**
Traveller status	
Traveller children	83.4
All other children	89.6
Immigrant status	
Immigrant children	82.9
All other children	89.7
Disability and/or Chronic Illness status	
Children with a disability and/or chronic illness	88.6
All other children	89.6

Source: HBSC Survey, Health Promotion Research Centre

Differences by age, gender, social class and over time

- The percentage of children who reported having 3 or more friends of the same gender was broadly similar across age, gender and social class categories, with no statistically significant differences (*see Table 36*).

Table 36: Percentage of children who report to have 3 or more friends of the same gender, by age, gender and social class (2002 and 2006)

	2002	2006		
	Total (%)	**Boys (%)**	**Girls (%)**	**Total (%)**
All children	**85.3**	**88.8**	**90.1**	**89.5**
Age				
9	–	94.3	94.1	94.2
10-11	85.1	88.4	90.2	89.5
12-14	85.7	89.9	90.9	90.3
15-17	85.7	88.1	89.6	88.8
Social class				
SC 1-2	86.8	88.5	90.8	89.6
SC 3-4	86.2	89.8	90.4	90.1
SC 5-6	84.5	90.3	90.7	90.4

Source: HBSC Survey, Health Promotion Research Centre

Differences by geographic location

- Children in the Mid-West region were more likely to report having 3 or more friends of the same gender (92.1%), while children in the West region were least likely to report this (87.4%) (*see Table 37*). These differences were not statistically significant.

Table 37: Percentage of children who report to have 3 or more friends of the same gender, by NUTS Region (2006)	
	%
All children	**89.5**
NUTS Region	
Border	90.9
Dublin	87.9
Midlands	88.5
Mid-East	90.6
Mid-West	92.1
South-East	90.3
South-West	90.2
West	87.4

Source: HBSC Survey, Health Promotion Research Centre

International comparisons

- From the 2006 HBSC Survey, using the ages of 11, 13 and 15 only to draw international comparisons, 86.4% of children from Ireland reported having 3 or more friends of the same gender (*see Figure 7*). This was significantly higher than the HBSC average of 79.0%.
- Among all 41 countries and regions that used this HBSC item, the lowest percentage for this indicator was found among Greek children (54.8%) and the highest among children from Hungary (89.1%). Overall, children from Ireland ranked 7th.

Figure 7: Percentage of children who report to have 3 or more friends of the same gender, by country (2006)

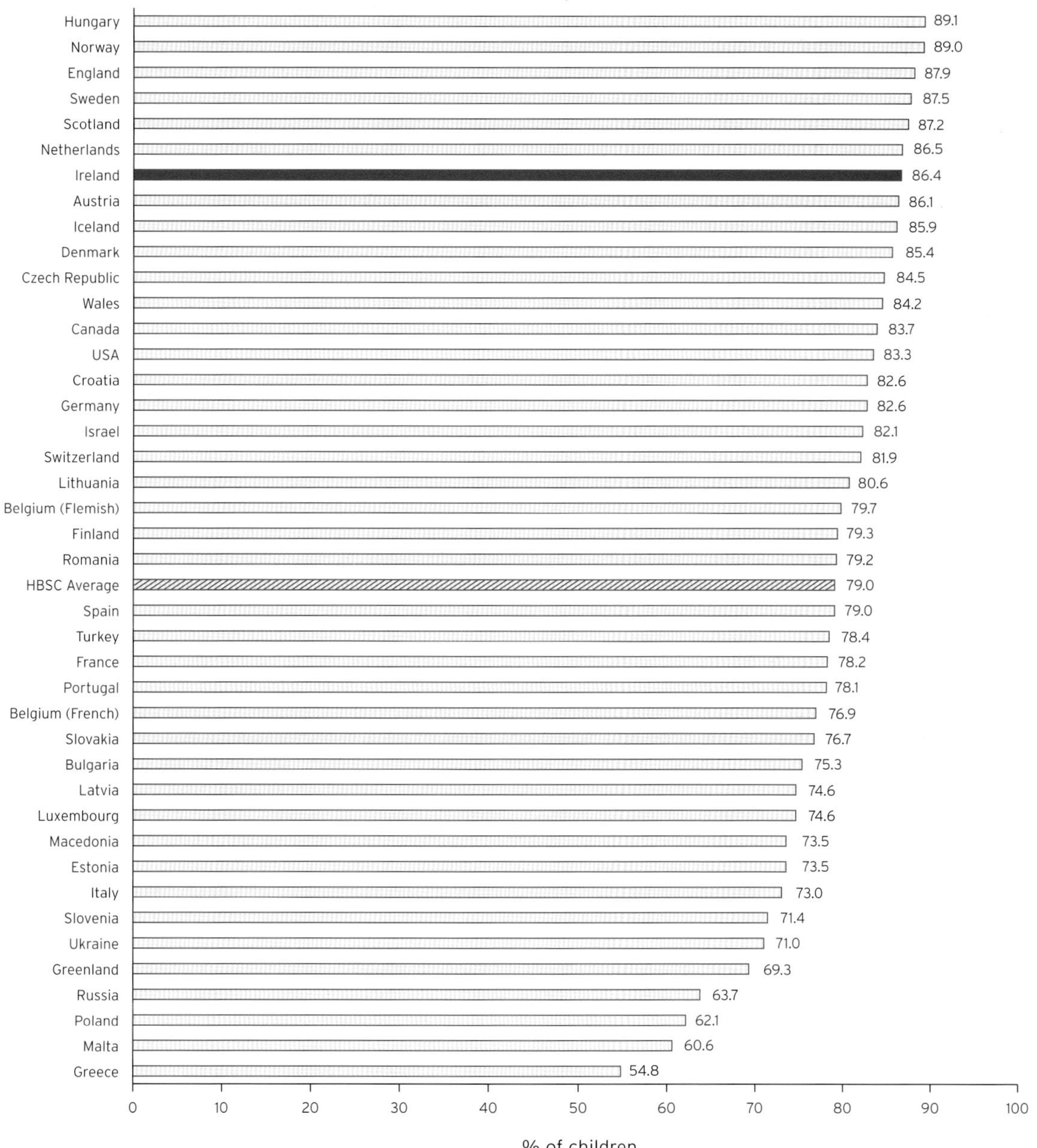

Source: HBSC Survey, Health Promotion Research Centre

PETS AND ANIMALS

The percentage of children who report to have a pet of their own or a pet in their family is significantly lower among Traveller children and immigrant children.

Measure

The percentage of children aged 9-17 who report having a pet of their own or a pet in their family.

Key findings

- In 2006, 73.8% of children aged 9-17 reported having a pet of their own or a pet in their family.

Differences by population groups

- When compared to other children, Traveller children and immigrant children were less likely to report having a pet of their own or a pet in their family (*see Table 38*). These differences were statistically significant.
- There were no significant differences between children with and children without a disability and/or chronic illness.

Table 38: Percentage of children who report having a pet of their own or a pet in their family, by population groups (2006)

	%
All children	**73.8**
Traveller status	
Traveller children	67.4
All other children	74.1
Immigrant status	
Immigrant children	58.2
All other children	74.6
Disability and/or Chronic Illness status	
Children with a disability and/or chronic illness	73.6
All other children	73.8

Source: HBSC Survey, Health Promotion Research Centre

Differences by age, gender and social class

- Statistically significant differences were also observed across gender and social class categories, with a lower percentage of boys and a lower percentage of children in the lowest social class category reporting to have a pet of their own or a pet in their family (*see Table 39*).
- The percentage of children in each age category who reported having a pet of their own or a pet in their family was broadly similar, with no statistical significant differences.

Table 39: Percentage of children who report having a pet of their own or a pet in their family, by age, gender and social class (2006)

	Boys (%)	Girls (%)	Total (%)
All children	**72.4**	**75.2**	**73.8**
Age			
9	71.1	72.9	72.0
10-11	71.6	77.3	75.0
12-14	73.6	75.2	74.4
15-17	71.6	74.3	72.9
Social class			
SC 1-2	74.4	78.7	76.4
SC 3-4	71.9	73.7	72.8
SC 5-6	72.9	74.8	73.9

Source: HBSC Survey, Health Promotion Research Centre

Differences by geographic location

- Children in the Mid-West region were more likely to report having a pet of their own or a pet in the family (80.2%), while children in the Dublin region were least likely to report this (62.8%) (*see Table 40*). These differences were statistically significant.

Table 40: Percentage of children who report having a pet of their own or a pet in their family, by NUTS Region (2006)

	%
All children	**73.8**
NUTS Region	
Border	71.3
Dublin	62.8
Midlands	78.2
Mid-East	76.8
Mid-West	80.2
South-East	79.9
South-West	76.6
West	75.8

Source: HBSC Survey, Health Promotion Research Centre

BULLYING

Immigrant children and children with a disability and/or chronic illness are more likely to report having been bullied at school.

Measure

The percentage of children aged 9-17 who report having been bullied at school.

Key findings

- In 2006, 24.5% of children aged 9-17 reported that they were bullied at school at least once in the past couple of months.

Differences by population groups

- When compared to other children, immigrant children and children with a disability and/or chronic illness were more likely to report that they were bullied at school (*see Table 41*). These differences were statistically significant.
- There were no significant differences between Traveller and non-Traveller children.

Table 41: Percentage of children who report having been bullied at school (in the past couple of months), by population groups (2006)

	%
All children	**24.5**
Traveller status	
Traveller children	28.8
All other children	24.3
Immigrant status	
Immigrant children	29.5
All other children	24.2
Disability and/or Chronic Illness status	
Children with a disability and/or chronic illness	29.9
All other children	23.1

Source: HBSC Survey, Health Promotion Research Centre

Differences by age, gender, social class and over time

- Statistically significant differences were also observed across age and gender, with a higher percentage of younger children and a higher percentage of boys reporting that they were bullied at school (*see Table 42*).
- The percentage of children in each social class category who reported being bullied at school was broadly similar, with no statistical significant differences.

Table 42: Percentage of children who report having been bullied at school (in the past couple of months), by age, gender and social class (1998, 2002 and 2006)

	1998	2002	2006		
	Total (%)	Total (%)	Boys (%)	Girls (%)	Total (%)
All children	**24.6**	**23.3**	**25.6**	**23.4**	**24.5**
Age					
9	–	–	38.4	38.1	38.3
10-11	31.2	28.3	27.9	30.2	29.3
12-14	25.2	25.8	28.2	23.9	26.2
15-17	18.8	18.2	22.1	19.5	20.8
Social class					
SC 1-2	21.8	23.0	26.5	23.5	25.0
SC 3-4	25.4	22.9	24.9	22.9	23.9
SC 5-6	24.3	23.1	26.0	23.3	24.6

Source: HBSC Survey, Health Promotion Research Centre

Differences by geographic location

- Children in the South-East and Mid-East regions were more likely to report being bullied at school (26.9%), while children in the Midlands were least likely to report this (22.9%) (*see Table 43*). These differences were statistically significant.

Table 43: Percentage of children who report having been bullied at school (in the past couple of months), by NUTS Region (2006)	
	%
All children	**24.5**
NUTS Region	
Border	23.8
Dublin	23.7
Midlands	22.9
Mid-East	26.9
Mid-West	23.2
South-East	26.9
South-West	23.2
West	24.0

Source: HBSC Survey, Health Promotion Research Centre

International comparisons

- From the 2006 HBSC Survey, using the ages of 11, 13 and 15 only to draw international comparisons, 25.9% of children from Ireland reported that they had been bullied at school at least once in the past couple of months (*see Figure 8*). This was significantly lower than the HBSC average of 32.0%.
- Among all 39 countries and regions that used this HBSC item, the lowest percentage for this indicator was found among children from Spain (13.6%) and the highest among children from Lithuania (56.3%). Overall, children from Ireland ranked 26th.

Figure 8: Percentage of children who report having been bullied at school (in the past couple of months), by country (2006)

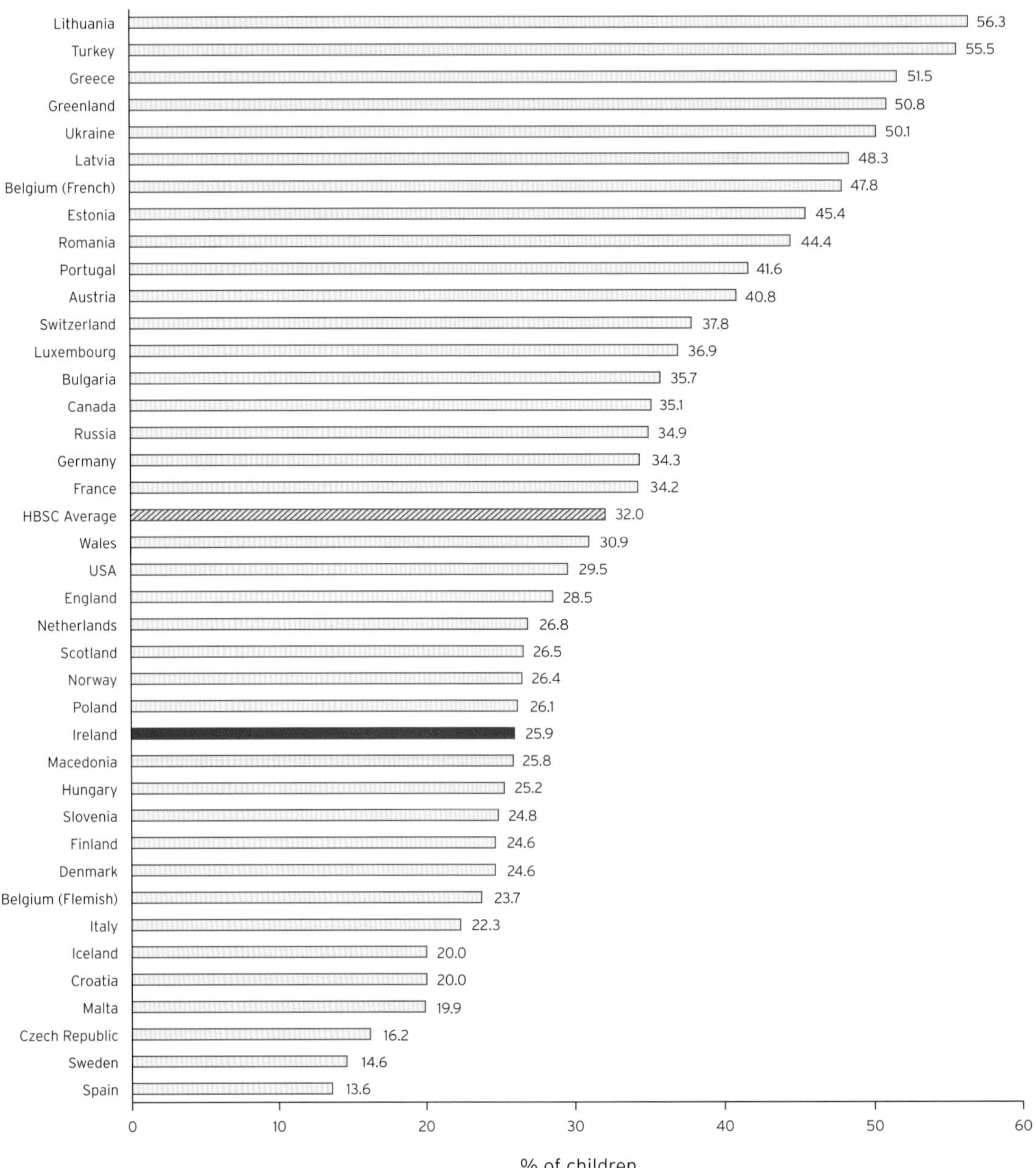

Source: HBSC Survey, Health Promotion Research Centre

PART 3: CHILDREN'S OUTCOMES

covering
Education
Health
Social, emotional and behavioural outcomes

EDUCATION OUTCOMES

ENROLMENT IN EARLY CHILDHOOD CARE AND EDUCATION

Almost one in 3 children under 13 years of age avails of non-parental childcare.

Measure

The percentage of children under 13 years of age who avail of non-parental childcare.

Key findings

- In 2007, 30% of children under 13 years of age availed of non-parental childcare.

Differences by age and household structure

- Pre-school children (42%) were more likely to avail of non-parental childcare when compared to primary school children (22%) (*see Table 44*).
- Pre-school children in two-parent households (44%) were more likely to avail of some form of non-parental childcare when compared with pre-school children in one-parent households (33%).

Table 44: Percentage of children under 13 years of age who avail of non-parental childcare, by school-going status and household structure (2007)

	Pre-school children	Primary school children	All children under 13 years
Total	**42**	**22**	**30**
Household structure			
One-parent households	33	25	28
Two-parent households	44	21	30

Source: Childcare Module, Quarterly National Household Survey, CSO

Differences by geographic location

- The highest proportion of children under 13 years of age availing of non-parental childcare was in the South-East region (34%) (*see Table 45*).

Table 45: Percentage of children under 13 years of age who avail of non-parental childcare, by school-going status and NUTS Region (2007)

	Pre-school children	Primary school children	All children under 13 years
Total	**42**	**22**	**30**
NUTS Region			
Border	38	20	27
Dublin	41	21	29
Midlands	44	18	28
Mid-East	43	24	31
Mid-West	41	27	32
South-East	44	28	34
South-West	41	21	28
West	43	18	28

Source: Childcare Module, Quarterly National Household Survey, CSO

PARENTAL SATISFACTION WITH EARLY CHILDHOOD CARE AND EDUCATION

Households in the Mid-West region are most likely to report that they have access to high-quality, affordable childcare in the community.

Measure

The percentage of households with children under 13 years of age who report they have 'access to high-quality, affordable childcare in the community'.

Key findings

- In 2007, 29% of households with children under 13 reported that they have access to high-quality, affordable childcare in the community.

Differences by household structure

- 23% of one-parent households reported to have access to high-quality, affordable childcare in the community, compared to 30% of two-parent households (*see Table 46*).

Table 46: Percentage of households with children under 13 who report they have 'access to high-quality, affordable childcare in the community', by household structure (2007)

	%
All households	**29**
Household structure	
One-parent households	23
Two-parent households	30

Source: Childcare Module, Quarterly National Household Survey, CSO

Differences by geographic location

- 45% of households in the Mid-West region reported that they have access to high-quality, affordable childcare in the community, compared to 21% of households in the Dublin region (*see Table 47*).
- Households in rural areas were more likely to report having access to high-quality, affordable childcare in the community when compared to households in urban areas (34% and 25% respectively).

Table 47: Percentage of households with children under 13 who report they have 'access to high-quality, affordable childcare in the community', by NUTS Region and location (2007)

	%
All households	**29**
NUTS Region	
Border	31
Dublin	21
Midlands	32
Mid-East	23
Mid-West	45
South-East	30
South-West	29
West	38
Location	
Rural	34
Urban	25

Source: Childcare Module, Quarterly National Household Survey, CSO

QUALITY OF EARLY CHILDHOOD CARE AND EDUCATION

82% of ECCE services under contract to deliver the Free Pre-School Year Scheme meet basic capitation criteria and 11% meet higher capitation criteria.

Measure

The percentage of Early Childhood Care and Education (ECCE) services under contract to deliver the Free Pre-School Year Scheme that meet basic and higher capitation criteria.

Key findings

- In June 2010, a total of 3,787 ECCE services were under contract to deliver the Free Pre-School Year Scheme. 82.0% met the basic capitation criteria and 11.0% met the higher capitation criteria.

Differences by geographic location

- Clare had the lowest proportion of ECCE services that met the basic capitation criteria (*see Table 48*).

Table 48: Percentage of Early Childhood Care and Education (ECCE) services under contract to deliver the Free Pre-School Year Scheme that meet basic and higher capitation criteria, by City and County Childcare Committees (2010)

	Total ECCE services	Meeting basic capitation criteria		Meeting higher capitation criteria	
	No.	No.	%	No.	%
State	**3,787**	**3,105**	**82.0**	**415**	**11.0**
City and County Childcare Committee					
Carlow	42	33	78.6	4	9.5
Cavan	55	43	78.2	7	12.7
Clare	130	91	70.0	2	1.5
Cork City	83	77	92.8	17	20.5
Cork County	292	272	93.2	56	19.2

continued

Table 48 ***(continued)***

City and County Childcare Committee	Total ECCE services	Meeting basic capitation criteria		Meeting higher capitation criteria	
	No.	No.	%	No.	%
Donegal	119	100	84.0	8	6.7
Dublin City	289	242	83.7	40	13.8
Dun Laoghaire/Rathdown	161	128	79.5	30	18.6
Fingal	277	200	72.2	28	10.1
Galway	242	195	80.6	19	7.9
Kerry	123	103	83.7	19	15.5
Kildare	206	161	78.2	22	10.7
Kilkenny	92	71	77.2	5	5.4
Laois	72	57	79.2	9	12.5
Leitrim	36	28	77.8	2	5.6
Limerick City	44	40	90.9	3	6.8
Limerick County	116	99	85.3	16	13.8
Longford	34	25	73.5	6	17.7
Louth	107	83	77.6	1	0.9
Mayo	108	102	94.4	6	5.6
Meath	183	143	78.1	15	8.2
Monaghan	55	49	89.1	7	12.7
Offaly	58	44	75.9	3	5.2
Roscommon	53	46	86.8	1	1.9
Sligo	60	43	71.7	5	8.3
South Dublin	190	157	82.6	15	7.9
Tipperary NR	70	65	92.9	10	14.3
Tipperary SR	68	53	77.9	9	13.2
Waterford City	38	37	97.4	3	7.9
Waterford County	47	44	93.6	2	4.3
Westmeath	81	68	84.0	17	21.0
Wexford	124	102	82.3	12	9.7
Wicklow	132	104	78.8	16	12.1

Source: ECCE Database, OMCYA

SCHOOL ATTENDANCE

One in every 8 primary school children and one in every 6 post-primary school children miss 20 days or more in the school year.

Measure

The percentage of children who are absent from school for 20 days or more in the school year.

Key findings

- In the 2007/08 school year, 12.0% of primary school children and 16.9% of post-primary school children were absent from school for 20 days or more (*see Table 49*).

Differences over age and time

- Over the period 2003/04 to 2007/08, the percentage of children who were absent from school for 20 days or more ranged between 11%-12% for primary school children and 16-18% for post-primary school children.

Table 49: Percentage of children who are absent from school for 20 days or more in the school year, by school-going status (2003/04 – 2007/08)

	2003/04	2004/05	2005/06	2006/07	2007/08
Primary school children	11.7	11.1	11.5	10.9	12.0
Post-primary school children	17.2	17.2	16.0	17.8	16.9

Source: National Educational Welfare Board

Differences by location and school type

- For primary schools, the average percentage of children missing 20 days or more was almost twice as high for schools in urban areas (15.1%) when compared to schools in rural areas (8.4%) (*see Table 50*). There was also a clear relationship between 20-day absences and levels of disadvantage. Using the Delivering Equality of Opportunity in Schools (DEIS) categories and participation in the School Support Programme (SSP), the average percentage of children missing 20 days or more tended to be higher in SSP schools when compared to non-SSP schools (although 20-day absences were still higher in non-SSP urban schools than in SSP rural schools).

- For post-primary schools, the average percentage of children missing 20 days or more was higher in Community/Comprehensive and Vocational schools. This was almost twice as high in DEIS schools (26.5%) when compared to non-DEIS schools (14.8%).

Table 50: Average percentage of children per school who are absent from school for 20 days or more in the school year, by selected school characteristics (2007/08)

	%
PRIMARY SCHOOL	
School location	
Rural	8.4
Urban	15.1
DEIS	
Rural, not in School Support Programme	8.0
Rural, in School Support Programme	10.3
Urban, not in School Support Programme	11.5
Urban, in School Support Programme Band 2	19.1
Urban, in School Support Programme Band 1	25.8
POST-PRIMARY SCHOOL	
Type of school	
Secondary	14.1
Community/Comprehensive	23.3
Vocational	23.0
DEIS	
DEIS	26.5
Non-DEIS	14.8

Source: National Educational Welfare Board

Differences by geographic location

- For primary schools, the average percentage of children missing 20 days or more was lowest in Monaghan (8.1%) and highest in Offaly (16.6%), while for post-primary schools the average percentage of children missing 20 days or more was lowest in Waterford (10.6%) and highest in Laois (23.6%) (*see Table 51*).

Table 51: Average percentage of children per school who are absent from school for 20 days or more in the school year, by school type and county (2007/08)

	Primary school	Post-primary school
Total	**12.1**	**19.2**
County		
Carlow	12.5	14.1
Cavan	10.8	23.5
Clare	9.4	12.8
Cork	9.6	14.9
Donegal	9.8	20.7
Dublin	14.8	19.6
Galway	12.1	18.2
Kerry	12.2	19.2
Kildare	11.8	15.3
Kilkenny	9.1	13.4
Laois	10.9	23.6
Leitrim	9.6	21.3
Limerick	12.9	14.6
Longford	13.1	21.9
Louth	12.9	16.8
Mayo	11.1	20.1
Meath	9.7	13.2
Monaghan	8.1	20.7
Offaly	16.6	20.7
Roscommon	10.0	18.9
Sligo	13.0	13.5
Tipperary NR	9.7	16.7
Tipperary SR	11.3	11.9
Waterford	12.1	10.6
Westmeath	11.7	16.2
Wexford	13.2	19.1
Wicklow	11.6	17.8

Source: National Educational Welfare Board

TRANSFER TO SECOND-LEVEL EDUCATION

The majority of children (98.5%) leaving national schools are known to have either progressed to another form of schooling or to have emigrated with their families.

Measure

The percentage of children leaving national schools, by destination.

Key findings

- In the 2009/10 school year, 94.3% of children leaving national schools are known to have progressed to another form of schooling (either at first or second level) and 4.2% of children are known to have emigrated with their families (*see Table 52*). Less than half of 1% of children leaving national schools were known not to have progressed to another school, while the destination of a further 1.2% of these children is unknown.

Differences by gender and over time

- Of the 278 children leaving national schools and not attending another school, 55.8% were boys and 44.2% were girls (*see Figure 9*).
- Over the 2005/06 - 2009/10 school years, approximately 95% of children leaving national schools are known to have progressed to another form of schooling (either at first or second level) and an increasing percentage of children are known to have emigrated with their families.

Table 52: Number and percentage of children leaving national schools, by destination (2005/06 – 2009/10)						
	2005/06	2006/07	2007/08	2008/09	2009/10	
	No.	No.	No.	No.	No.	%
Total number of children	**76,187**	**75,991**	**77,226**	**80,444**	**83,488**	**100.0**
Destination						
Attending another school within the State	73,331	72,566	73,420	75,823	78,703	94.3
Emigrating	2,050	2,260	2,657	3,280	3,474	4.2
Not attending another school	263	256	280	334	278	0.3
Unknown	543	909	869	1,007	1,033	1.2

Source: Education Statistics, Department of Education and Skills

Figure 9: Percentage of children leaving national schools and not attending another school, by gender (2005/06 - 2009/10)

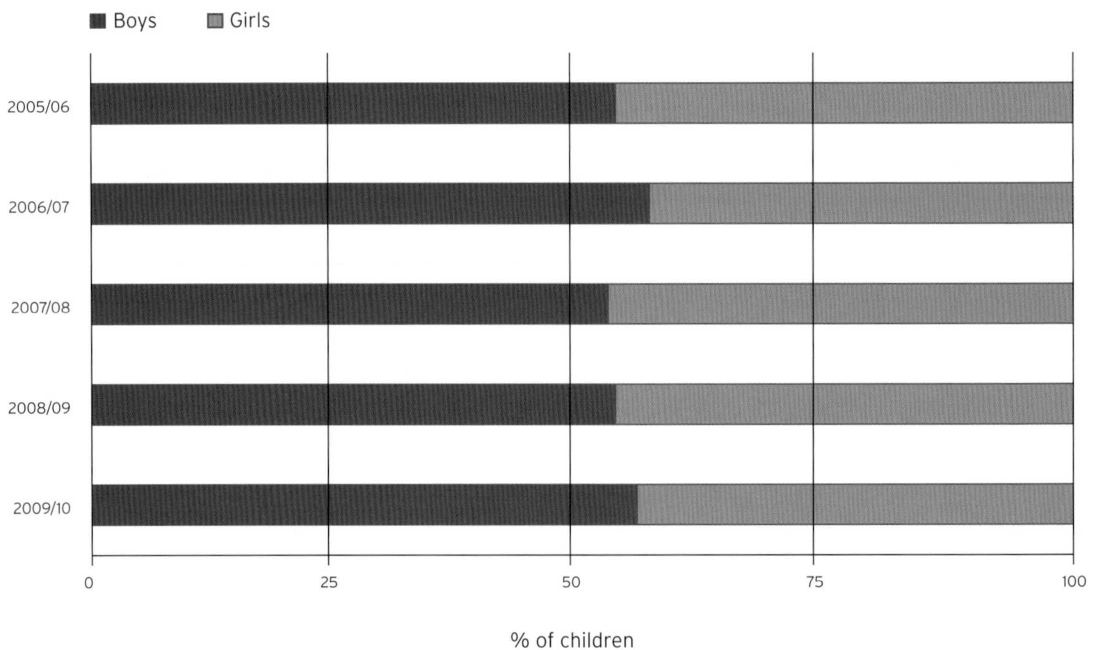

Source: Education Statistics, Department of Education and Skills

ACHIEVEMENT IN READING

There has been a significant decline in reading literacy scores among 15-year-olds in Ireland.

Measure

The mean scores of children aged 15 based on the OECD-PISA Reading Literacy Scale.

Key findings

- In 2009, children aged 15 in Ireland achieved a mean score of 495.6 on the OECD-PISA Reading Literacy Scale.

Differences by population groups

- The mean score on the OECD-PISA Reading Literacy Scale for immigrant children (473.1) was significantly lower than the corresponding mean score for all other children (501.9) (*see Table 53*).

Table 53: Mean score for children aged 15 based on the OECD-PISA Reading Literacy Scale, by population groups (2009)

	%	Mean score
All children	**100.0**	**495.6**
Immigrant status		
Immigrant children	8.3	473.1
All other children	91.7	501.9

Source: PISA Survey, Education Research Centre

Differences by gender, social class and over time

- Girls in Ireland performed significantly better in reading literacy than boys, achieving a mean score of 515.4 compared to 476.3 (*see Table 54*). There was also a large difference in favour of girls in 2006 and 2003.

- Reading achievement was related to social class across all three PISA cycles considered here. In 2009, the mean score of children from the highest social class category (535.5) was significantly higher than the mean score of children in the lowest social class category (459.5).
- The mean reading score for students in Ireland in 2009 (495.6) was significantly lower than the Irish mean score in 2000 (526.7), which was the last time reading was a major assessment domain in PISA, and was also lower than in 2003 (515.5) and 2006 (517.3).

Table 54: Mean score for children aged 15 based on the OECD-PISA Reading Literacy Scale, by gender and social class (2003, 2006 and 2009)

	2003	2006	2009
All children	**515.5**	**517.3**	**495.6**
Gender			
Boys	501.1	500.2	476.3
Girls	530.1	534.0	515.4
Social class			
High SES	547.8	551.2	535.5
Medium SES	521.6	522.4	497.9
Low SES	484.3	490.2	459.5

Source: PISA Survey, Education Research Centre

International comparisons

- In 2009, Ireland's mean score of 495.6 on the OECD-PISA Reading Literacy Scale was not significantly different from the OECD mean score of 493.4 (*see Figure 10*).
- Mexico was the lowest-scoring OECD country on this indicator, while Korea achieved the highest mean score.
- Ireland ranked 17th (true rank: 12th – 22nd) in reading literacy among the 34 participating OECD countries. Ireland's mean score was not significantly different from those of 13 other OECD countries, including Norway, Poland, USA, Germany, France and United Kingdom.

Figure 10: Mean scores of children aged 15 based on the OECD-PISA Reading Literacy Scale, by OECD country (2009)

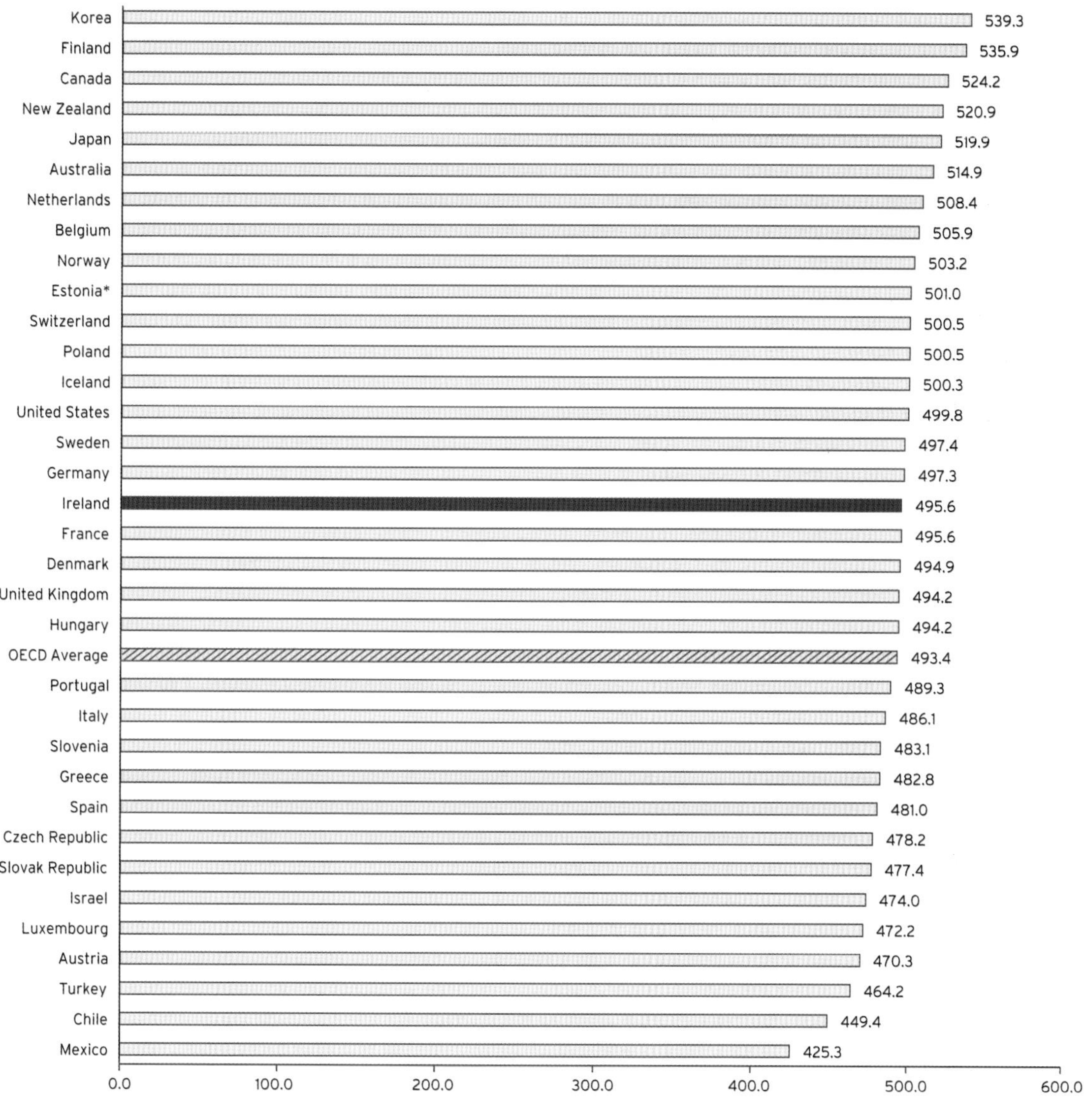

* PISA 2009 data for Estonia (an accession candidate country) are included in the OECD average estimates.

Source: PISA Survey, Education Research Centre

ACHIEVEMENT IN MATHEMATICS

Mathematics literacy scores of 15-year-olds in Ireland are significantly below the OECD average.

Measure

The mean scores of children aged 15 based on the OECD-PISA Mathematics Literacy Scale.

Key findings

- In 2009, children aged 15 in Ireland achieved a mean score of 487.1 on the OECD-PISA Mathematics Literacy Scale.

Differences by population groups

- The mean score on the OECD-PISA Mathematics Literacy Scale for immigrant children (471.7) was significantly lower than the corresponding mean score for all other children (491.7) *(see Table 55)*.

Table 55: Mean score for children aged 15 based on the OECD-PISA Mathematics Literacy Scale, by population groups (2009)

	%	Mean score
All children	**100.0**	**487.1**
Immigrant status		
Immigrant children	8.3	471.7
All other children	91.7	491.7

Source: PISA Survey, Education Research Centre

Differences by gender, social class and over time

- Boys in Ireland achieved a higher mean score on the OECD-PISA Mathematics Literacy Scale than girls (490.9 compared to 483.3), although the difference was not significant (*see Table 56*). In both 2006 and 2003, boys significantly outscored girls.

- The mean mathematics score of children from the highest social class category (523.4) was significantly higher than the mean of children from the medium or lowest social class categories (490.1 and 452.3 respectively). Mathematics achievement was similarly related to social class in 2006 and 2003.
- The mean mathematics score for students in Ireland in 2009 (487.1) was significantly lower than the Irish mean score in 2003 (502.8), the last time mathematics was a major assessment domain in PISA.

Table 56: Mean score for children aged 15 based on the OECD-PISA Mathematics Literacy Scale, by gender and social class (2003, 2006 and 2009)

	2003	2006	2009
All children	**502.8**	**501.5**	**487.1**
Gender			
Boys	510.2	507.3	490.9
Girls	495.4	495.8	483.3
Social class			
High SES	535.7	532.8	523.4
Medium SES	506.1	505.0	490.1
Low SES	473.5	476.0	452.3

Source: PISA Survey, Education Research Centre

International comparisons

- In 2009, Ireland's mean score of 487.1 on the OECD-PISA Mathematics Literacy Scale was significantly below the OECD mean score of 495.7 *(see Figure 11)*.
- Mexico was the lowest-scoring OECD country on this indicator, while Korea achieved the highest mean score.
- Ireland ranked 26th (true rank: 22nd - 29th) in mathematical literacy among all 34 participating OECD countries. Ireland's mean score was not significantly different from the mean scores of 10 other OECD countries, including Sweden, Czech Republic, United Kingdom and USA.

Figure 11: Mean scores of children aged 15 based on the OECD-PISA Mathematics Literacy Scale, by OECD country (2009)

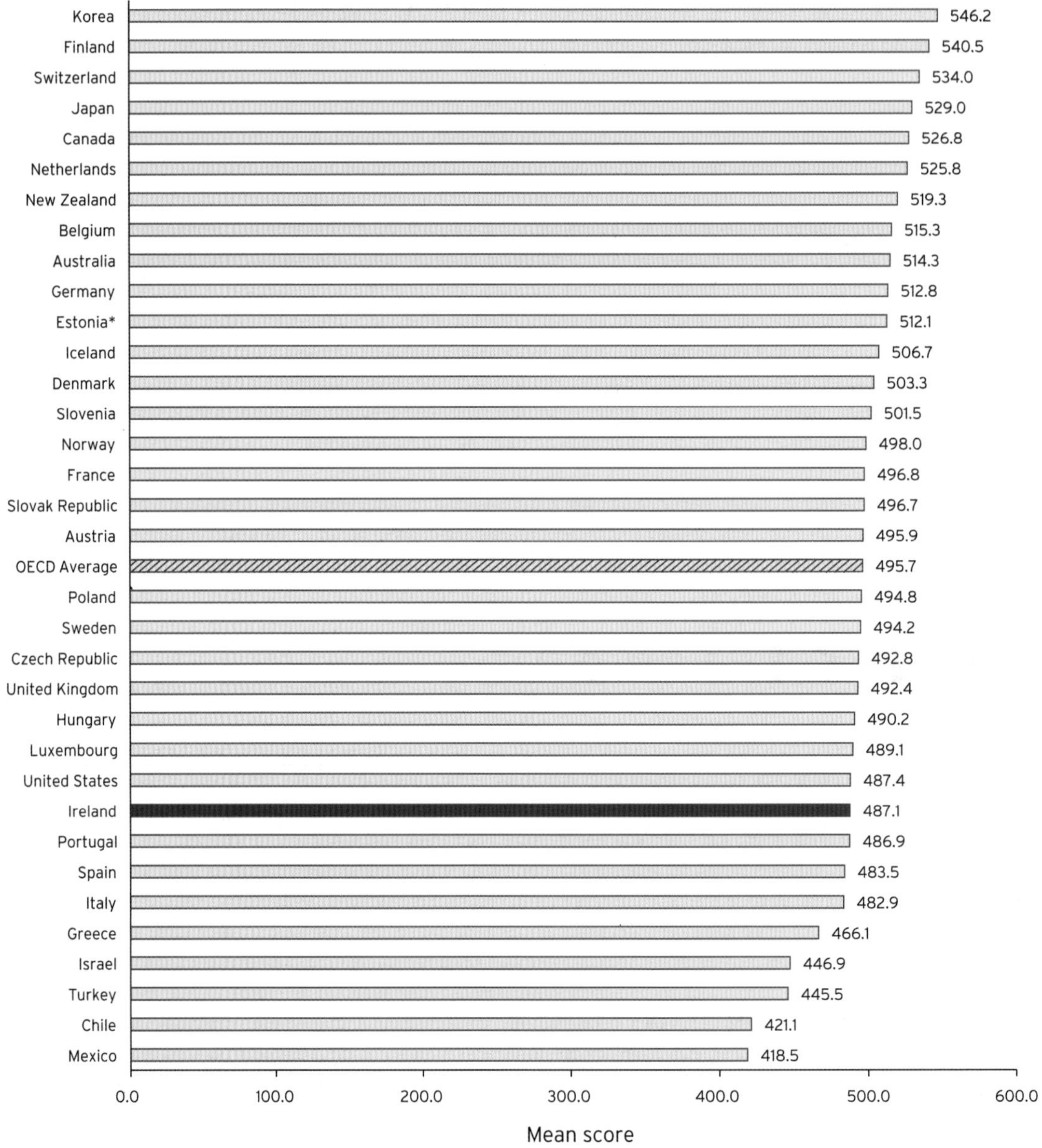

* PISA 2009 data for Estonia (an accession candidate country) are included in the OECD average estimates.

Source: PISA Survey, Education Research Centre

ACHIEVEMENT IN SCIENCE

Science literacy scores of 15-year-olds in Ireland are significantly above the OECD average.

Measure

The mean scores of children aged 15 based on the OECD-PISA Combined Scientific Literacy Scale.

Key findings

- In 2009, children aged 15 in Ireland achieved a mean score of 508.0 on the OECD-PISA Combined Scientific Literacy Scale.

Differences by population groups

- The mean score on the OECD-PISA Combined Scientific Literacy Scale for immigrant children (492.3) was significantly lower than the corresponding mean score for all other children (513.1) (*see Table 57*).

Table 57: Mean score for children aged 15 based on the OECD-PISA Combined Scientific Literacy Scale, by population groups (2009)

	%	Mean score
All children	**100.0**	**508.0**
Immigrant status		
Immigrant children	8.3	492.3
All other children	91.7	513.1

Source: PISA Survey, Education Research Centre

Differences by gender, social class and over time

- Girls in Ireland achieved a higher mean score on the OECD-PISA Combined Scientific Literacy Scale than boys (509.4 and 506.6 respectively), although this difference was not significant *(see Table 58)*. Similarly in 2006 and 2003, the mean scores of boys and girls did not differ significantly from each other.

- As with reading and mathematics in 2009, children from the highest social class category achieved a significantly higher mean score in science (545.7) than children in the medium or lowest social class categories (512.8 and 471.0 respectively). A similar pattern was observed in 2006 and 2003.
- The mean science score for students in Ireland in 2009 (508.0) was almost identical to the Irish mean score in 2006 (508.3), the last time science was a major assessment domain in PISA.

Table 58: Mean score for children aged 15 based on the OECD-PISA Combined Scientific Literacy Scale, by gender and social class (2003, 2006 and 2009)

	2003	2006	2009
All children	**505.4**	**508.3**	**508.0**
Gender			
Boys	506.4	508.1	506.6
Girls	504.4	508.5	509.4
Social class			
High SES	542.5	542.3	545.7
Medium SES	509.6	512.8	512.8
Low SES	470.8	480.7	471.0

Source: PISA Survey, Education Research Centre

International comparisons

- In 2009, Ireland's mean score of 508.0 on the OECD-PISA Combined Scientific Literacy Scale was significantly above the OECD mean score of 500.8 *(see Figure 12)*.
- Mexico was the lowest-scoring OECD country on this indicator, while Finland achieved the highest mean score.
- Ireland ranked 14th (true rank: 11th - 17th) in scientific literacy among all 34 participating OECD countries. Ireland's mean score was not significantly different from the mean scores of 8 other OECD countries, including the United Kingdom, USA, Czech Republic, Hungary and Norway.

Figure 12: Mean scores of children aged 15 based on the OECD-PISA Combined Scientific Literacy Scale, by OECD country (2009)

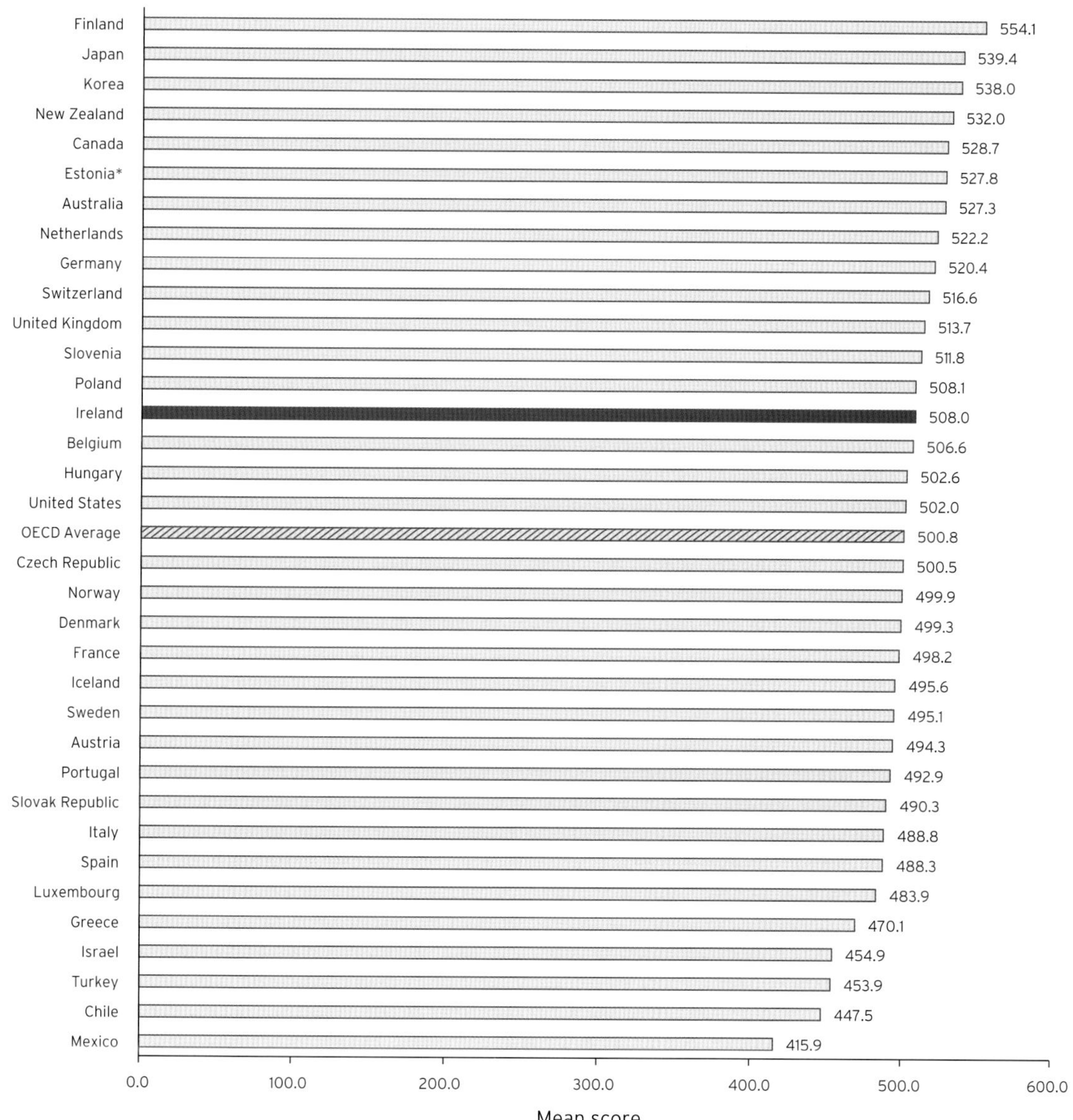

* PISA 2009 data for Estonia (an accession candidate country) are included in the OECD average estimates.

Source: PISA Survey, Education Research Centre

HEALTH OUTCOMES

BIRTH WEIGHT

The percentage of low birth weight babies has remained relatively stable over the last 5 years.

Measure

The percentage of babies born weighing less than 2,500 grams (live and still births).

Key findings

- In 2008, 5.6% of all babies born were in the low birth weight category (less than 2,500 grams).

Differences by gender, social class and over time

- Girls were more likely than boys to be born in the low birth weight category (6.0% and 5.2% respectively) (*see Table 59*).
- There were also marked social class differences (*see Figure 13*). The percentage of babies born in the low birth weight category were higher among mothers who reported to be 'unemployed' (9.0%) compared to mothers in 'higher professional' groups (4.1%).
- Over the period 2004-2008, the percentage of babies born in the low birth weight category has been relatively stable.

Table 59: Percentage of babies born weighing less than 2,500 grams (live and still births), by gender (2004-2008)

	2004	2005	2006	2007	2008		
	Low birth weight (%)	Low birth weight (%)	Low birth weight (%)	Low birth weight (%)	Low birth weight (%)	Healthy birth weight (%)	High birth weight (%)
Total	**5.3**	**5.3**	**5.3**	**5.6**	**5.6**	**78.2**	**16.2**
Gender							
Boys	5.1	4.9	5.0	5.1	5.2	75.2	19.5
Girls	5.5	5.8	5.6	6.0	6.0	81.3	12.6

Source: National Perinatal Reporting System, ESRI

Figure 13: Percentage of babies born weighing less than 2,500 grams (live and still births), by occupation of mother (2008)*

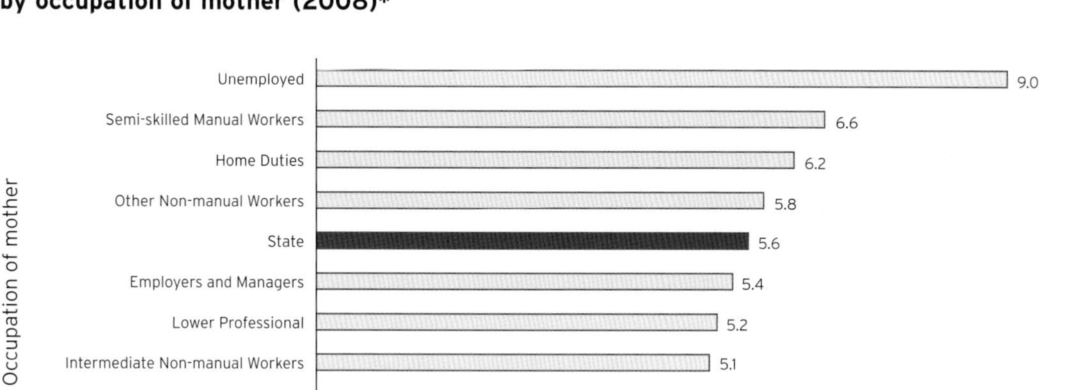

* Categories where percentages are based on less than 100 births (i.e. 'unskilled manual workers', 'other agricultural occupations and fishermen', 'farmers and farm managers') and 'not stated' and 'not classifiable' categories have been omitted from this Figure.

Source: National Perinatal Reporting System, ESRI

Differences by geographic location

- Waterford had the highest proportion of babies born in the low birth weight category (*see Table 60*).

Table 60: Number and percentage of babies born weighing less than 2,500 grams (live and still births), by mothers' county of residence (2008)*		
	No.	Low birth weight births as % of all births
Total	**4,251**	**5.6**
County		
Carlow	67	6.2
Cavan	58	4.6
Clare	111	6.0
Cork	485	5.8
Donegal	101	4.5
Dublin City	885	5.9
Dublin County	294	5.2
Galway	234	5.6
Kerry	102	4.9
Kildare	212	5.3
Kilkenny	80	5.7
Laois	89	6.5
Leitrim	27	5.2
Limerick	193	6.0
Longford	43	5.9
Louth	114	5.7
Mayo	84	4.4
Meath	200	5.5
Monaghan	48	5.5
Offaly	68	5.5
Roscommon	52	5.7
Sligo	34	3.5
Tipperary NR	67	6.7
Tipperary SR	78	5.3
Waterford	142	7.1
Westmeath	79	5.2
Wexford	151	6.0
Wicklow	146	5.8

* Categories where percentages are based on less than 100 births (i.e. 7 births with 'other' place of residence for mother) have been omitted from this Table.

Source: National Perinatal Reporting System, ESRI

BREASTFEEDING

Breastfeeding initiation rates have continued to increase.

Measure

The percentage of infants who are (a) exclusively breastfed and (b) who are partially breastfed on discharge from hospital.

Key findings

- In 2008, 50.9% of infants were breastfed on discharge from hospital. This includes 44.3% who were exclusively breastfed and a further 6.6% who were fed using a combination of bottle and breastfeeding.

Differences by age, social class and over time

- The percentage of infants who were breastfed (either exclusive or combined) is higher among older mothers (*see Table 61*). 26.9% of mothers aged 15-19 breastfed their infants compared to 57.7% of mothers aged 45 or more.
- There were also marked social class differences (*see Figure 14*). The percentage of infants who were breastfed (either exclusive or combined) was higher among mothers in 'higher' and 'lower professional' groups (69.1% and 67.2% respectively) compared to mothers who reported to be 'unemployed' (35.3%).
- Over the period 2004-2008, the percentage of infants who were breastfed (either exclusive or combined) on discharge from hospital has risen consistently.

Table 61: Percentage of infants who are breastfed (exclusive or combined) on discharge from hospital, by mothers' age (2004-2008)*

	2004		2005		2006		2007		2008		
	Exclusive	Combined	Exclusive	Combined	Exclusive	Combined	Exclusive	Combined	Exclusive	Combined	Total
Total	**42.1**	**3.3**	**43.8**	**3.7**	**44.1**	**4.6**	**44.9**	**5.5**	**44.3**	**6.6**	**50.9**
Age											
15-19	20.1	2.4	22.1	2.3	20.9	2.6	22.9	3.6	22.2	4.7	26.9
20-24	29.7	2.5	32.4	2.9	36.0	3.5	36.7	5.0	35.5	5.9	41.4
25-29	41.0	3.6	41.9	3.8	42.3	4.4	43.9	5.8	44.1	6.9	51.0
30-34	45.5	3.5	47.4	3.9	47.2	5.0	47.7	5.6	47.3	6.9	54.2
35-39	48.8	3.3	49.2	3.7	48.7	4.8	48.8	5.5	47.1	6.4	53.5
40-44	49.5	3.4	51.0	4.1	50.0	4.8	50.3	6.0	48.5	7.7	56.2
Over 45	56.5	3.2	44.4	6.2	58.8	8.8	50.9	4.4	49.7	8.0	57.7

* Categories where percentages are based on less than 100 births (i.e. 'under 15 years' and 'age not stated') have been omitted from this Table.

Source: National Perinatal Reporting System, ESRI

Figure 14: Percentage of infants who are breastfed (either exclusive or combined) on discharge from hospital, by mothers' occupation (2008)*

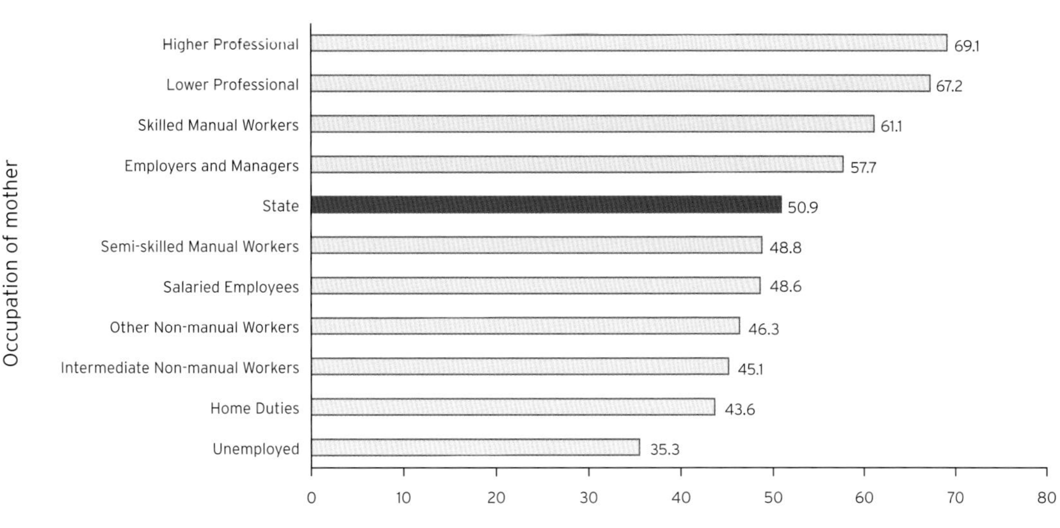

* Categories where percentages are based on less than 100 births (i.e. 'unskilled manual workers', 'other agricultural occupations and fishermen', 'farmers and farm managers') and 'not stated' and 'not classifiable' categories have been omitted from this Figure.

Source: National Perinatal Reporting System, ESRI

Differences by geographic location

- Dublin County had the highest proportion of infants who were breastfed (either exclusive or combined) on discharge from hospital (*see Table 62*).

Table 62: Percentage of infants who are breastfed (exclusive or combined) on discharge from hospital, by mothers' county of residence (2008)*			
	Exclusive	**Combined**	**Total**
	%	%	%
Total	**44.3**	**6.6**	**50.9**
County			
Carlow	48.4	1.5	49.9
Cavan	45.3	3.4	48.7
Clare	20.3	3.7	24.0
Cork	41.2	10.8	52.0
Donegal	30.2	7.9	38.1
Dublin City	50.7	6.5	57.2
Dublin County	55.7	7.0	62.7
Galway	33.2	21.6	54.8
Kerry	43.2	7.3	50.5
Kildare	49.9	4.8	54.7
Kilkenny	53.5	0.6	54.1
Laois	50.4	3.2	53.6
Leitrim	46.2	8.5	54.7
Limerick	19.0	1.7	20.7
Longford	46.6	3.4	50.0
Louth	42.3	6.1	48.4
Mayo	48.3	4.2	52.5
Meath	49.4	5.5	54.9
Monaghan	41.9	4.2	46.1
Offaly	44.8	2.0	46.8
Roscommon	46.3	5.9	52.2
Sligo	35.4	9.6	45.0
Tipperary NR	26.2	1.4	27.6
Tipperary SR	45.7	0.4	46.1
Waterford	48.4	2.6	51.0
Westmeath	50.3	3.4	53.7
Wexford	39.1	4.8	43.9
Wicklow	51.0	5.8	56.8

* Categories where percentages are based on less than 100 births (i.e. 'other' and 'not stated') have been omitted from this Table.

Source: National Perinatal Reporting System, ESRI

HEALTH CONDITIONS AND HOSPITALISATION

More than half of the total hospital discharges among children were children under 5 years of age.

Measure

The number of hospital discharges among children.

Key findings

- In 2009, there was a total of 145,749 hospital discharges among children.

Differences by age, gender, principal diagnosis and over time

- More than half of the total hospital discharges were among infants and children aged 1-4 years old (22.5% and 29.6% respectively) and more than half of the total hospital discharges were among boys (55.4%) (*see Table 63*).
- The most common reported principal diagnosis recorded was 'diseases of the respiratory system' (13.0%), followed by 'injury, poisoning and certain other consequences of external causes' (9.7%).
- Over the period 2005-2009, the total number of hospital discharges and the most common reported principal diagnosis have remained relatively stable.

Table 63: Number and percentage of hospital discharges among children, by age, gender and principal diagnosis (2005-2009)

	2005	2006	2007	2008	2009	
	No.	No.	No.	No.	No.	%
Total	**142,245**	**146,187**	**145,051**	**145,649**	**145,749**	**100.0**
Age						
Under 1	30,283	31,687	31,614	33,478	32,863	22.5
1-4	42,154	43,662	42,659	42,258	43,206	29.6
5-9	28,079	28,717	28,210	28,184	28,657	19.7
10-14	23,564	23,396	22,865	23,551	22,538	15.5
15-17	18,165	18,725	19,703	18,178	18,485	12.7
Gender						
Boys	78,503	82,239	80,925	81,462	80,752	55.4
Girls	63,742	63,948	64,126	64,187	64,997	44.6
Principal diagnosis (Top 10)						
Diseases of the respiratory system	21,931	22,167	19,897	18,608	18,969	13.0
Injury, poisoning and certain other consequences of external causes	15,256	14,905	15,105	14,221	14,159	9.7
Diseases of the digestive system	12,493	12,791	12,815	13,127	13,144	9.0
Certain infectious and parasitic diseases	11,764	13,485	13,187	12,357	11,858	8.1
Certain conditions originating in the perinatal period	8,688	9,295	9,261	9,503	9,818	6.7
Congenital malformations, deformations and chromosomal abnormalities	8,004	8,251	8,682	9,094	9,142	6.3
Diseases of the genitourinary system	7,401	7,280	7,615	7,716	7,910	5.4
Neoplasms	6,402	6,319	6,046	6,157	5,827	4.0
Diseases of the ear and mastoid process	5,551	5,475	4,723	5,044	4,865	3.3
Diseases of the skin and subcutaneous tissue	4,051	3,821	4,095	4,141	4,002	2.7
All other conditions and reasons for admission	40,704	42,398	43,625	45,681	46,055	31.6

Source: Hospital In-Patient Enquiry, Department of Health and Children

Differences by geographic location

- Almost one-quarter (23.2%) of the total hospital discharges among children were among children resident in Dublin (*see Table 64*).

Table 64: Number and percentage of hospital discharges among children, by county of residence (2009)

	No.	%
Total	**145,749**	**100.0**
County		
Carlow	1,880	1.3
Cavan	2,449	1.7
Clare	3,452	2.4
Cork	15,369	10.5
Donegal	6,405	4.4
Dublin	33,753	23.2
Galway	8,662	5.9
Kerry	4,038	2.8
Kildare	7,061	4.8
Kilkenny	2,587	1.8
Laois	2,967	2.0
Leitrim	887	0.6
Limerick	6,878	4.7
Longford	1,402	1.0
Louth	3,948	2.7
Mayo	5,768	4.0
Meath	5,351	3.7
Monaghan	1,674	1.1
Offaly	3,061	2.1
Roscommon	2,311	1.6
Sligo	2,768	1.9
Tipperary NR	2,343	1.6
Tipperary SR	3,219	2.2
Waterford	3,955	2.7
Westmeath	4,030	2.8
Wexford	4,999	3.4
Wicklow	4,104	2.8
Non-resident	428	0.3

Source: Hospital In-Patient Enquiry, Department of Health and Children

ACCIDENTS, INJURIES AND HOSPITALISATION

The number of hospital discharges among children with a diagnosis of 'transport accidents', 'intentional self-harm' and 'accidental poisoning' continues to decrease.

Measure

The number of hospital discharges among children with a diagnosis of external causes of injury or poisoning.

Key findings

- In 2009, there was a total of 14,159 hospital discharges among children with a diagnosis of 'external causes of injury or poisoning'.

Differences by age, gender, principal diagnosis and over time

- Almost one-third (30.8%) of the hospital discharges with a diagnosis of 'external causes of injury or poisoning' were among children aged 1-4 and 62.2% of these hospital discharges were among boys (*see Figure 15*).
- Over the period 2005-2009, the total number of hospital discharges among children with a diagnosis of 'external causes of injury or poisoning' has fallen consistently (*see Table 65*). More specifically, the number of hospital discharges among children with a diagnosis of 'transport accidents', 'intentional self-harm' and 'accidental poisoning' has fallen over this period.

Table 65: Number and percentage of hospital discharges among children with a diagnosis of external causes of injury or poisoning, by age, gender and cause (2005-2009)

	2005	2006	2007	2008	2009	
	No.	No.	No.	No.	No.	%
Total	**15,256**	**14,905**	**15,105**	**14,221**	**14,159**	**100.0**
Age						
Under 1	786	830	895	971	972	6.9
1-4	4,217	4,322	4,236	4,069	4,367	30.8
5-9	3,578	3,571	3,629	3,294	3,380	23.9
10-14	3,676	3,335	3,458	3,347	3,001	21.2
15-17	2,999	2,847	2,887	2,540	2,439	17.2
Gender						
Boys	9,418	9,271	9,474	8,931	8,803	62.2
Girls	5,838	5,634	5,631	5,290	5,356	37.8
Principal diagnosis						
Accidental falls	6,107	6,067	5,973	5,664	5,884	41.6
Accidents caused by objects*	2,318	2,456	2,538	2,243	2,141	15.1
Transport accidents	1,944	1,770	1,758	1,606	1,476	10.4
Accident, not otherwise specified	381	441	527	549	605	4.3
Drowning, submersion, other accidental threats to breathing and foreign bodies	377	544	571	540	539	3.8
Accidental poisoning	503	427	454	427	340	2.4
Intentional self-harm	401	385	352	359	321	2.3
Assault	300	318	317	345	295	2.1
Contact with heat or hot substances	243	302	289	256	272	1.9
Event of undetermined intent	114	103	105	100	87	0.6
Exposure to smoke, fire and flames	64	113	74	51	55	0.4
Other external causes of injury	1,466	1,769	2,033	2,014	2,079	14.7
External cause not reported**	1,038	210	114	67	65	0.5

* 'Accidents caused by objects' include striking against or being struck accidentally by objects or persons; caught accidentally in or between objects; accidents caused by machinery; and accidents caused by cutting/piercing objects.

** 'External cause not reported' refers to discharges with a principal diagnosis of 'Injury, poisoning and certain other consequences of external causes', and for which an external cause of injury or poisoning was not recorded. The inclusion of this category ensures that the total reported corresponds with the data reported for 'Injury, poisoning and certain other consequences of external causes' in Table 63.

Source: Hospital In-Patient Enquiry, Department of Health and Children

Figure 15: Number of hospital discharges among children with a diagnosis of external causes of injury or poisoning, by age and gender (2009)

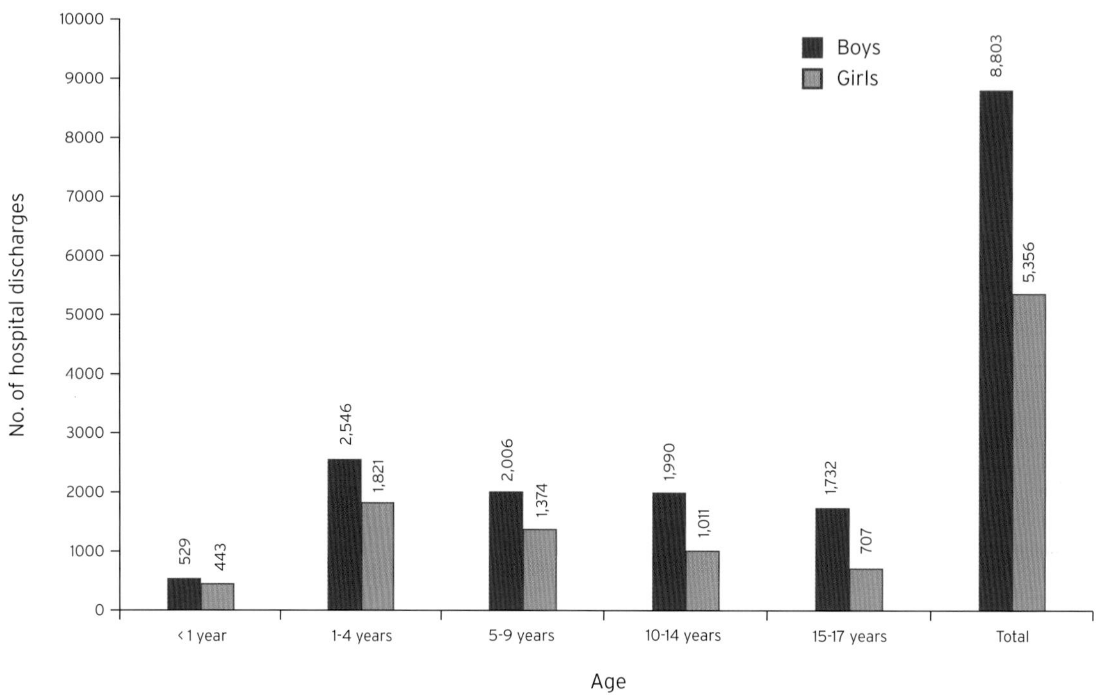

Source: Hospital In-Patient Enquiry, Department of Health and Children

Differences by geographic location

- Over one in 4 (25.8%) of the total hospital discharges among children with a diagnosis of external causes of injury or poisoning were among children resident in Dublin (*see Table 66*).

Table 66: Number and percentage of hospital discharges among children with a diagnosis of external causes of injury or poisoning, by county of residence (2009)

	No.	%
Total	**14,159**	**100.0**
County		
Carlow	189	1.3
Cavan	275	1.9
Clare	314	2.2
Cork	1,467	10.4
Donegal	529	3.7
Dublin	3,649	25.8
Galway	864	6.1
Kerry	435	3.1
Kildare	700	4.9
Kilkenny	268	1.9
Laois	213	1.5
Leitrim	66	0.5
Limerick	552	3.9
Longford	139	1.0
Louth	422	3.0
Mayo	401	2.8
Meath	577	4.1
Monaghan	149	1.1
Offaly	247	1.7
Roscommon	184	1.3
Sligo	212	1.5
Tipperary NR	177	1.3
Tipperary SR	306	2.2
Waterford	389	2.7
Westmeath	342	2.4
Wexford	528	3.7
Wicklow	473	3.3
Non-resident	92	0.6

Source: Hospital In-Patient Enquiry, Department of Health and Children

NUTRITIONAL OUTCOMES

Almost one-quarter of 7-year-old children are either overweight or obese.

Measure

The percentage of children aged 7 in the Body Mass Index (BMI) categories of normal, overweight and obese.

Key findings

- In 2008, 77% of children aged 7 were classified in the 'normal' weight category according to the International Obesity Taskforce Standards. The remaining 23% of children were classified as either 'overweight' or 'obese' (16% and 7% respectively).

Differences by gender

- Boys (82%) were more likely than girls (73%) to be categorised in the 'normal' weight category (*see Table 67*). 18% of boys were categorised as either 'overweight' or 'obese' (13% and 5% respectively), while 27% of girls were categorised as either 'overweight' or 'obese' (19% and 8% respectively).

Table 67: Percentage of children aged 7 in the BMI categories of normal, overweight and obese, by gender (2008)

	Normal	Overweight	Obese
	%	%	%
Total	**77**	**16**	**7**
Gender			
Boys	82	13	5
Girls	73	19	8

Source: WHO European Childhood Obesity Surveillance Initiative, National Nutrition Surveillance Centre

INTELLECTUAL DISABILITY

Approximately 6 in 10 children registered as having an intellectual disability are boys.

Measure

The number of children registered as having an intellectual disability.

Key findings

- In 2009, there were 8,028 children registered as having an intellectual disability. This equates to an overall rate of 72.5 children per 10,000.

Differences by age, gender, severity of disability and over time

- 14.4% (1,159) of children registered as having an intellectual disability were aged 0-4 years; 30.2% (2,428) were aged 5-9; 34.0% (2,732) were aged 10-14; and the remaining 21.3% (1,709) were aged 15-17 *(see Table 68)*.
- 62.9% (5,051) of children registered as having an intellectual disability were boys and 37.1% (2,977) were girls. This equates to a rate of 89.0 per 10,000 boys and 55.2 per 10,000 girls.
- The majority of children were registered as having a mild or moderate disability (37.2% and 29.7% respectively).
- Over the period 2005-2009, the number of children under 18 years registered as having an intellectual disability increased consistently. However, this number fell slightly in 2009.

Table 68: Number, percentage and rate (per 10,000) of children under 18 years registered as having an intellectual disability, by age, gender and severity of disability (2005-2009)

	2005	2006	2007	2008	2009		
	No.	No.	No.	No.	No.	%	Rate per 10,000
Total	**7,385**	**7,658**	**7,802**	**8,095**	**8,028**	**100.0**	**72.5**
Age							
0-4	1,127	1,085	1,071	1,272	1,159	14.4	33.9
5-9	2,049	2,357	2,468	2,470	2,428	30.2	78.8
10-14	2,400	2,400	2,519	2,636	2,732	34.0	94.8
15-17	1,809	1,816	1,744	1,717	1,709	21.3	101.0
Gender							
Boys	4,523	4,858	4,898	5,077	5,051	62.9	89.0
Girls	2,862	2,800	2,904	3,018	2,977	37.1	55.2
Severity of disability							
Mild	3,013	2,912	2,870	3,001	2,983	37.2	26.9
Moderate	2,098	2,113	2,134	2,323	2,386	29.7	21.6
Severe	778	775	740	782	785	9.8	7.1
Profound	151	150	147	153	175	2.2	1.6
Not verified	1,345	1,708	1,911	1,836	1,699	21.1	15.3

Source: National Intellectual Disability Database, Health Research Board

Differences by geographic location

- 19.2% (1,538) of children registered as having an intellectual disability resided in Dublin North East, 27.4% (2,199) resided in Dublin Mid-Leinster, 29.9% (2,399) resided in the South and the remaining 23.6% (1,891) resided in the West (*see Table 69*).

Table 69: Number and percentage of children under 18 years registered as having an intellectual disability, by HSE Region and Local Health Office (LHO) Area (2009)

	No.	%
Total	**8,028**	**100.0**
HSE Dublin North East	**1,538**	**19.2**
Cavan/Monaghan	163	2.0
Dublin North	404	5.0
Dublin North Central	169	2.1
Dublin North West	247	3.1
Louth	303	3.8
Meath	252	3.1
HSE Dublin Mid-Leinster	**2,199**	**27.4**
Dublin South	275	3.4
Dublin South City	90	1.1
Dublin South East	81	1.0
Dublin South West	236	2.9
Dublin West	408	5.1
Kildare/West Wicklow	405	5.0
Laois/Offaly	221	2.8
Longford/Westmeath	228	2.8
Wicklow	255	3.2
HSE South	**2,399**	**29.9**
Carlow/Kilkenny	366	4.6
Kerry	293	3.6
North Cork	218	2.7
North Lee	405	5.0
South Lee	111	1.4
Tipperary SR	298	3.7
Waterford	282	3.5
West Cork	139	1.7
Wexford	287	3.6

continued

Table 69 *(continued)*		
	No.	**%**
HSE West	**1,891**	**23.6**
Clare	117	1.5
Donegal	316	3.9
Galway	503	6.3
Limerick	216	2.7
Mayo	246	3.1
Roscommon	168	2.1
Sligo/Leitrim/West Cavan	208	2.6
Tipperary NR	117	1.5
Outside Ireland	<5	0.0

Source: National Intellectual Disability Database, Health Research Board

PHYSICAL AND SENSORY DISABILITY

Approximately one in 4 children on the National Physical and Sensory Disability Database are registered as having multiple disabilities.

Measure

The number of children under 18 years registered as having a physical and/or sensory disability.

Key findings

- In 2009, there were 8,043 children under 18 years registered as having a physical and/or sensory disability. This equates to an overall rate of 72.7 children per 10,000.

Differences by age, gender, type of disability and over time

- 6.3% (510) of children registered as having a physical and/or sensory disability were aged 0-4 years; 33.6% (2,700) were aged 5-9; 42.1% (3,387) were aged 10-14; and the remaining 18.0% (1,446) were aged 15-17 *(see Table 70).*
- 62.5% (5,027) of children registered as having a physical and/or sensory disability were boys and 37.5% (3,016) were girls. This equates to a rate of 88.6 per 10,000 boys and 55.9 per 10,000 girls.
- The majority of children were registered as having either a physical disability or a speech and language disability (36.5% and 29.1% respectively), while 28.2% of children were registered as having multiple disabilities.
- Over the period 2005-2009, the number of children under 18 years registered as having a physical and/or sensory disability increased consistently. However, this number fell slightly in 2009.

Table 70: Number, percentage and rate (per 10,000) of children under 18 years registered as having a physical and/or sensory disability, by age, gender and type of disability (2005-2009)

	2005	2006	2007	2008	2009		
	No.	No.	No.	No.	No.	%	Rate per 10,000
Total	**7,039**	**7,807**	**8,373**	**8,546**	**8,043**	**100.0**	**72.7**
Age							
0-4	754	712	697	640	510	6.3	14.9
5-9	2,808	2,987	3,081	2,994	2,700	33.6	87.7
10-14	2,435	2,841	3,189	3,466	3,387	42.1	117.6
15-17	1,042	1,267	1,406	1,446	1,446	18.0	85.4
Gender							
Boys	4,343	4,840	5,213	5,348	5,027	62.5	88.6
Girls	2,696	2,967	3,160	3,198	3,016	37.5	55.9
Type of disability							
Physical	5,485	5,704	5,463	3,235	2,939	36.5	26.5
Hearing loss/deafness	450	447	425	328	287	3.6	2.6
Visual	228	245	233	213	211	2.6	1.9
Speech and language	300	533	1,121	2,538	2,339	29.1	21.1
Multiple disabilities	575	877	1,130	2,231	2,266	28.2	20.5
Refused	<5	<5	<5	<5	<5	0.0	0.0

Source: National Physical and Sensory Disability Database, Health Research Board

Differences by geographic location

- 9.5% (768) of children registered as having a physical and/or sensory disability resided in Dublin North East, 30.1% (2,418) resided in Dublin Mid-Leinster, 30.0% (2,412) resided in the South and the remaining 30.4% (2,445) resided in the West (*see Table 71*).

Table 71: Number and percentage of children under 18 years registered as having a physical and/or sensory disability, by HSE Region and Local Health Office (LHO) Area (2009)

	No.	%
Total	**8,043**	**100.0**
HSE Dublin North East	**768**	**9.5**
Cavan/Monaghan	145	1.8
Dublin North	117	1.5
Dublin North Central	53	0.7
Dublin North West	98	1.2
Louth	183	2.3
Meath	172	2.1
HSE Dublin Mid-Leinster	**2,418**	**30.1**
Dublin South	135	1.7
Dublin South City	148	1.8
Dublin South East	109	1.4
Dublin South West	253	3.1
Dublin West	512	6.4
Kildare/West Wicklow	370	4.6
Laois/Offaly	229	2.8
Longford/Westmeath	397	4.9
Wicklow	265	3.3
HSE South	**2,412**	**30.0**
Carlow/Kilkenny	361	4.5
Kerry	251	3.1
North Cork	170	2.1
North Lee	464	5.8
South Lee	525	6.5
Tipperary SR	194	2.4
Waterford	179	2.2
West Cork	126	1.6
Wexford	142	1.8

continued

Table 71 *(continued)*		
	No.	**%**
HSE West	**2,445**	**30.4**
Clare	160	2.0
Donegal	218	2.7
Galway	626	7.8
Limerick	234	2.9
Mayo	675	8.4
Roscommon	260	3.2
Sligo/Leitrim/West Cavan	125	1.6
Tipperary NR	147	1.8

Source: National Physical and Sensory Disability Database, Health Research Board

CHILD WELFARE AND PROTECTION: INITIAL ASSESSMENT

The number of child welfare and protection reports that went to initial assessment increased by 2,844 over the period 2006-2008.

Measure

The number of child welfare and protection reports that went to initial assessment.

Key findings

- In 2008, there were 15,364 child welfare and protection reports that went to initial assessment.

Differences by type of concern and over time

- Almost half (48.9%) of the child welfare and protection reports that went to initial assessment were for welfare concerns (*see Table 72*).
- Over the period 2006-2008, the number of child welfare and protection reports that went to initial assessment has increased.

Table 72: Number and percentage of child welfare and protection reports that went to initial assessment, by type of concern (2006-2008)

	2006	2007*	2008	
	No.	No.	No.	%
Total	**12,520**	**15,074**	**15,364**	**100.0**
Type of concern				
Welfare	6,221	7,690	7,518	48.9
Physical abuse	1,291	1,529	1,704	11.1
Sexual abuse	1,495	1,715	1,657	10.8
Emotional abuse	1,100	1,233	1,270	8.3
Neglect	2,413	2,907	3,215	20.9

* excludes Waterford Local Health Office returns.

Source: Child Care Interim Data Set, HSE

Differences by geographic location

- The highest number and percentage of cases that went to initial assessment for child welfare and protection concerns was in the Longford/ Westmeath Local Health Office (LHO) Area in the HSE Dublin Mid-Leinster Region (*see Table 73*).

Table 73: Number and percentage of child welfare and protection reports that went to initial assessment, by type of concern, HSE Region and Local Health Office (LHO) Area (2008)

	Welfare	Physical abuse	Sexual abuse	Emotional abuse	Neglect	Total	
	No.	No.	No.	No.	No.	No.	%
Total	**7,518**	**1,704**	**1,657**	**1,270**	**3,215**	**15,364**	**100.0**
HSE Dublin North East	**1,353**	**409**	**458**	**227**	**881**	**3,328**	**21.7**
Cavan/Monaghan	94	29	54	25	116	318	2.1
Dublin North	379	82	135	28	135	759	4.9
Dublin North Central	214	43	67	28	142	494	3.2
Dublin North West	389	102	90	26	170	777	5.1
Louth	259	106	95	90	274	824	5.4
Meath	18	47	17	30	44	156	1.0
HSE Dublin Mid-Leinster	**2,710**	**750**	**624**	**475**	**1,238**	**5,797**	**37.7**
Dublin South	82	28	35	5	35	185	1.2
Dublin South City	155	42	83	5	134	419	2.7
Dublin South East	231	49	75	21	68	444	2.9
Dublin South West	466	90	111	21	172	860	5.6
Dublin West	232	147	79	24	205	687	4.5
Kildare/West Wicklow	259	67	58	22	57	463	3.0
Laois/Offaly	586	135	74	90	161	1,046	6.8
Longford/Westmeath	540	148	69	273	344	1,374	8.9
Wicklow	159	44	40	14	62	319	2.1

continued

Table 73 *(continued)*

	Welfare	Physical abuse	Sexual abuse	Emotional abuse	Neglect	Total	
	No.	No.	No.	No.	No.	No.	%
HSE South	**1,624**	**288**	**327**	**274**	**568**	**3,081**	**20.1**
Carlow/Kilkenny	126	40	30	16	62	274	1.8
Kerry	198	25	37	30	64	354	2.3
North Cork	154	13	23	20	60	270	1.8
North Lee	82	15	12	7	17	133	0.9
South Lee	21	12	0	4	15	52	0.3
Tipperary SR	445	34	41	33	164	717	4.7
Waterford	81	51	52	29	24	237	1.5
West Cork	124	15	26	27	47	239	1.6
Wexford	393	83	106	108	115	805	5.2
HSE West	**1,831**	**257**	**248**	**294**	**528**	**3,158**	**20.6**
Clare	301	38	53	20	105	517	3.4
Donegal	26	6	6	4	5	47	0.3
Galway	0	35	15	61	87	198	1.3
Limerick	633	66	79	25	76	879	5.7
Mayo	73	28	35	19	80	235	1.5
Roscommon	162	20	21	113	107	423	2.8
Sligo/Leitrim/West Cavan	49	18	4	8	9	88	0.6
Tipperary NR	587	46	35	44	59	771	5.0

Source: Child Care Interim Data Set, HSE

CHILD WELFARE AND PROTECTION: CONFIRMED ABUSE

The number of cases of confirmed child abuse has increased by 367 cases over the period 2006-2008.

Measure

The number of confirmed child abuse cases.

Key findings

- In 2008, there were 2,164 confirmed cases of abuse.

Differences by type of abuse and over time

- The majority of confirmed child abuse cases were for cases of neglect (44.6%), followed by cases of physical abuse (22.0%) (*see Table 74*).
- Over the period 2006-2008, the number of confirmed child abuse cases has increased.

Table 74: Number and percentage of confirmed child abuse cases, by type of abuse (2006-2008)

	2006	2007*	2008	
	No.	No.	No.	%
Total	**1,797**	**1,978**	**2,164**	**100.0**
Type of abuse				
Physical abuse	352	389	476	22.0
Sexual abuse	275	293	289	13.4
Emotional abuse	375	432	434	20.1
Neglect	795	864	965	44.6

* excludes Waterford Local Health Office returns.

Source: Child Care Interim Data Set, HSE

Differences by geographic location

- The highest number and percentage of confirmed child abuse cases was in the Longford/Westmeath Local Health Office (LHO) Area in the HSE Dublin Mid-Leinster Region (*see Table 75*).

Table 75: Number and percentage of confirmed child abuse cases, by type of abuse, HSE Region and Local Health Office (LHO) Area (2008)

	Physical abuse	Sexual abuse	Emotional abuse	Neglect	Total	
	No.	No.	No.	No.	No.	%
Total	**476**	**289**	**434**	**965**	**2,164**	**100.0**
HSE Dublin North East	**107**	**54**	**40**	**186**	**387**	**17.9**
Cavan/Monaghan	0	0	0	0	0	0.0
Dublin North	47	26	16	95	184	8.5
Dublin North Central	19	8	10	14	51	2.4
Dublin North West	29	15	5	41	90	4.2
Louth	2	1	2	16	21	1.0
Meath	10	4	7	20	41	1.9
HSE Dublin Mid-Leinster	**284**	**124**	**252**	**505**	**1,165**	**53.8**
Dublin South	1	3	0	0	4	0.2
Dublin South Central	36	16	5	38	95	4.4
Dublin South East	2	2	0	3	7	0.3
Dublin South West	65	38	24	94	221	10.2
Dublin West	67	19	2	84	172	7.9
Kildare/West Wicklow	37	28	50	92	207	9.6
Laois/Offaly	15	5	4	22	46	2.1
Longford/Westmeath	57	8	165	166	396	18.3
Wicklow	4	5	2	6	17	0.8

continued

Table 75 *(continued)*						
	Physical abuse	Sexual abuse	Emotional abuse	Neglect	Total	
	No.	No.	No.	No.	No.	%
HSE South	**35**	**68**	**29**	**90**	**222**	**10.3**
Carlow/Kilkenny	5	8	1	7	21	1.0
Kerry	1	6	3	6	16	0.7
North Cork	1	0	0	2	3	0.1
North Lee	8	4	10	5	27	1.2
South Lee	1	0	0	0	1	0.0
Tipperary SR	3	3	3	35	44	2.0
Waterford	4	9	3	7	23	1.1
West Cork	1	8	3	9	21	1.0
Wexford	11	30	6	19	66	3.0
HSE West	**50**	**43**	**113**	**184**	**390**	**18.0**
Clare	2	3	1	15	21	1.0
Donegal	0	1	0	1	2	0.1
Galway	16	6	37	28	87	4.0
Limerick	7	8	4	27	46	2.1
Mayo	11	14	1	24	50	2.3
Roscommon	8	7	54	61	130	6.0
Sligo/Leitrim/West Cavan	0	1	7	4	12	0.6
Tipperary NR	6	3	9	24	42	1.9

Source: Child Care Interim Data Set, HSE

SOCIAL, EMOTIONAL AND BEHAVIOURAL OUTCOMES

PARTICIPATION IN DECISION-MAKING

The percentage of children who report that students at their school participate in making the school rules has decreased from approximately 33% in 1998 to 23% in 2006.

Measure

The percentage of children aged 9-17 who report that students at their school participate in making the school rules.

Key findings

- In 2006, 22.5% of children aged 9-17 reported that students at their school participate in making the school rules.

Differences by population groups

- When compared to other children, Traveller children and children with a disability and/or chronic illness were more likely to report that students in their school participate in making the school rules (*see Table 76*). These differences were statistically significant.
- There were no significant differences between immigrant and non-immigrant children.

Table 76: Percentage of children who report that students at their school participate in making the school rules, by population groups (2006)

	%
All children	**22.5**
Traveller status	
Traveller children	32.5
All other children	22.1
Immigrant status	
Immigrant children	22.7
All other children	22.5
Disability and/or Chronic Illness status	
Children with a disability and/or chronic illness	24.6
All other children	21.8

Source: HBSC Survey, Health Promotion Research Centre

Differences by age, gender, social class and over time

- Statistically significant differences were also observed across age and social class categories, with a higher percentage of younger children and a higher percentage of children in the lowest social class category reporting that students in their school participate in making the school rules (*see Table 77*).
- There were no significant differences between boys and girls.

Table 77: Percentage of children who report that students at their school participate in making the school rules, by age, gender and social class (1998, 2002 and 2006)

	1998	2002	2006		
	Total (%)	Total (%)	Boys (%)	Girls (%)	Total (%)
All children	**32.5**	**23.5**	**21.9**	**23.1**	**22.5**
Age					
9	–	–	42.3	43.6	42.9
10-11	39.5	36.0	33.2	42.5	38.7
12-14	34.2	25.6	24.6	23.6	24.1
15-17	24.7	14.6	15.9	14.0	15.0
Social class					
SC 1-2	28.8	21.5	19.2	20.0	19.6
SC 3-4	33.6	23.5	21.8	22.8	22.3
SC 5-6	34.2	26.8	22.7	25.4	24.1

Source: HBSC Survey, Health Promotion Research Centre

Differences by geographic location

- Children in the Dublin region were more likely to report that students at their school participate in making the school rules (28.1%), while children in the Mid-West region were least likely to report this (17.2%) (*see Table 78*). These differences were statistically significant.

Table 78: Percentage of children who report that students at their school participate in making the school rules, by NUTS Region (2006)

	%
All children	**22.5**
NUTS Region	
Border	21.5
Dublin	28.1
Midlands	21.3
Mid-East	19.4
Mid-West	17.2
South-East	20.0
South-West	24.1
West	19.4

Source: HBSC Survey, Health Promotion Research Centre

International comparisons

- From the 2006 HBSC Survey, using the ages of 11, 13, and 15 only to draw international comparisons, 24.9% of children from Ireland reported that students in their school participate in making the school rules (*see Figure 16*). This was significantly lower than the HBSC average of 33.8%.
- Among the 7 countries and regions that used this HBSC item, the lowest percentage for this indicator was found among children from Ireland (24.9%) and the highest among children from Macedonia (50.3%).

Figure 16: Percentage of children who report that students at their school participate in making the school rules, by country (2006)

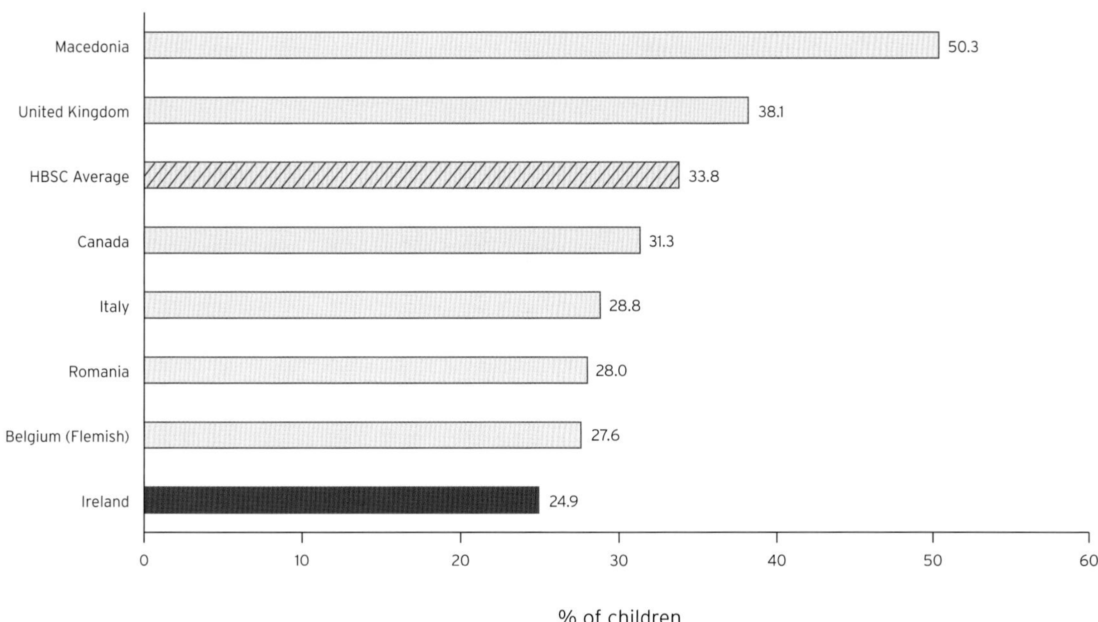

Source: HBSC Survey, Health Promotion Research Centre

READING AS A LEISURE ACTIVITY

Approximately one-third of 15-year-old children report that reading is one of their favourite hobbies.

Measure

The percentage of children aged 15 who report that reading is one of their favourite hobbies.

Key findings

- In 2009, 31.7% of children aged 15 reported that reading was one of their favourite hobbies.

Differences by population groups

- When compared to other children, Traveller children were less likely to report that reading was one of their favourite hobbies (*see Table 79*). This difference was statistically significant.
- There was no significant difference between immigrant and non-immigrant children.

Table 79: Percentage of children aged 15 who report that reading is one of their favourite hobbies, by population groups (2009)

	%
All children	**31.7**
Traveller status	
Traveller children	19.9
All other children	32.0
Immigrant status	
Immigrant children	43.7
All other children	31.1

Source: PISA Survey, Education Research Centre

Differences by gender, social class and over time

- The percentage of girls (40.2%) who reported that reading was one of their favourite hobbies was significantly higher than the corresponding percentage of boys (23.4%) (*see Table 80*).
- Children in the lowest social class category (25.3%) were significantly less likely to report that reading was one of their favourite hobbies when compared to children in the highest and medium social class categories (39.2% and 31.7% respectively).
- In 2009, the percentage of children (31.7%) who reported that reading was one of their favourite hobbies was significantly lower than the corresponding percentages in 2006 (42.6%) and 2000 (35.7%).

Table 80: Percentage of children aged 15 who report that reading is one of their favourite hobbies, by gender and social class (2000, 2006 and 2009)

	2000	2006	2009
All children	**35.7**	**42.6**	**31.7**
Gender			
Boys	22.9	32.7	23.4
Girls	48.2	52.0	40.2
Social class			
High SES	40.7	50.0	39.2
Medium SES	35.0	41.8	31.7
Low SES	30.8	36.5	25.3

Source: PISA Survey, Education Research Centre

SMOKING CIGARETTES

Daily cigarette smoking is significantly higher among Traveller children.

Measure

The percentage of children aged 9-17 who report smoking cigarettes every day.

Key findings

- In 2006, 8.5% of children aged 9-17 reported smoking cigarettes every day.

Differences by population groups

- When compared to other children, Traveller children were more likely to report that they smoked cigarettes every day (*see Table 81*). This difference was statistically significant.
- There were no significant differences between immigrant and non-immigrant children or between children with and children without a disability and/or chronic illness.

Table 81: Percentage of children who report smoking cigarettes every day, by population groups (2006)

	%
All children	**8.5**
Traveller status	
Traveller children	16.0
All other children	8.5
Immigrant status	
Immigrant children	9.5
All other children	8.5
Disability and/or Chronic Illness status	
Children with a disability and/or chronic illness	9.0
All other children	8.4

Source: HBSC Survey, Health Promotion Research Centre

Differences by age, gender, social class and over time

- Statistically significant differences were also observed across age and social class categories, with a higher percentage of older children and a higher percentage of children in the lowest social class category reporting to smoke cigarettes every day (*see Table 82*).
- There were no significant differences between boys and girls.

Table 82: Percentage of children who report smoking cigarettes every day, by age, gender and social class (1998, 2002 and 2006)

	1998	2002	2006		
	Total (%)	Total (%)	Boys (%)	Girls (%)	Total (%)
All children	**9.7**	**10.0**	**8.3**	**8.8**	**8.5**
Age					
9	–	–	0.3	0.1	0.2
10-11	0.5	0.4	1.1	0.3	0.6
12-14	7.3	5.7	4.6	4.7	4.6
15-17	19.7	19.7	14.4	17.0	15.6
Social class					
SC 1-2	8.2	7.2	5.9	7.2	6.5
SC 3-4	9.4	9.5	7.7	9.3	8.5
SC 5-6	9.7	10.4	7.9	8.3	8.1

Source: HBSC Survey, Health Promotion Research Centre

Differences by geographic location

- Children in the Midlands region were more likely to report smoking cigarettes every day (14.3%), while children in the South-West were least likely to report this (6.3%) (*see Table 83*). These differences were statistically significant.

Table 83: Percentage of children who report smoking cigarettes every day, by NUTS Region (2006)	
	%
All children	**8.5**
NUTS Region	
Border	6.8
Dublin	9.8
Midlands	14.3
Mid-East	9.2
Mid-West	7.8
South-East	8.5
South-West	6.3
West	9.1

Source: HBSC Survey, Health Promotion Research Centre

International comparisons

- From the 2006 HBSC Survey, using the ages of 11, 13 and 15 only to draw international comparisons, 6.5% of children from Ireland reported smoking cigarettes every day (*see Figure 17*). This was significantly higher than the HBSC average of 5.8%.
- Among all 40 countries and regions that used this HBSC item, the lowest percentage for this indicator was found among children from Sweden (2.2%) and the highest among children from Greenland (14.2%). Overall, children from Ireland ranked 17th.

Figure 17: Percentage of children who report smoking cigarettes every day, by country (2006)

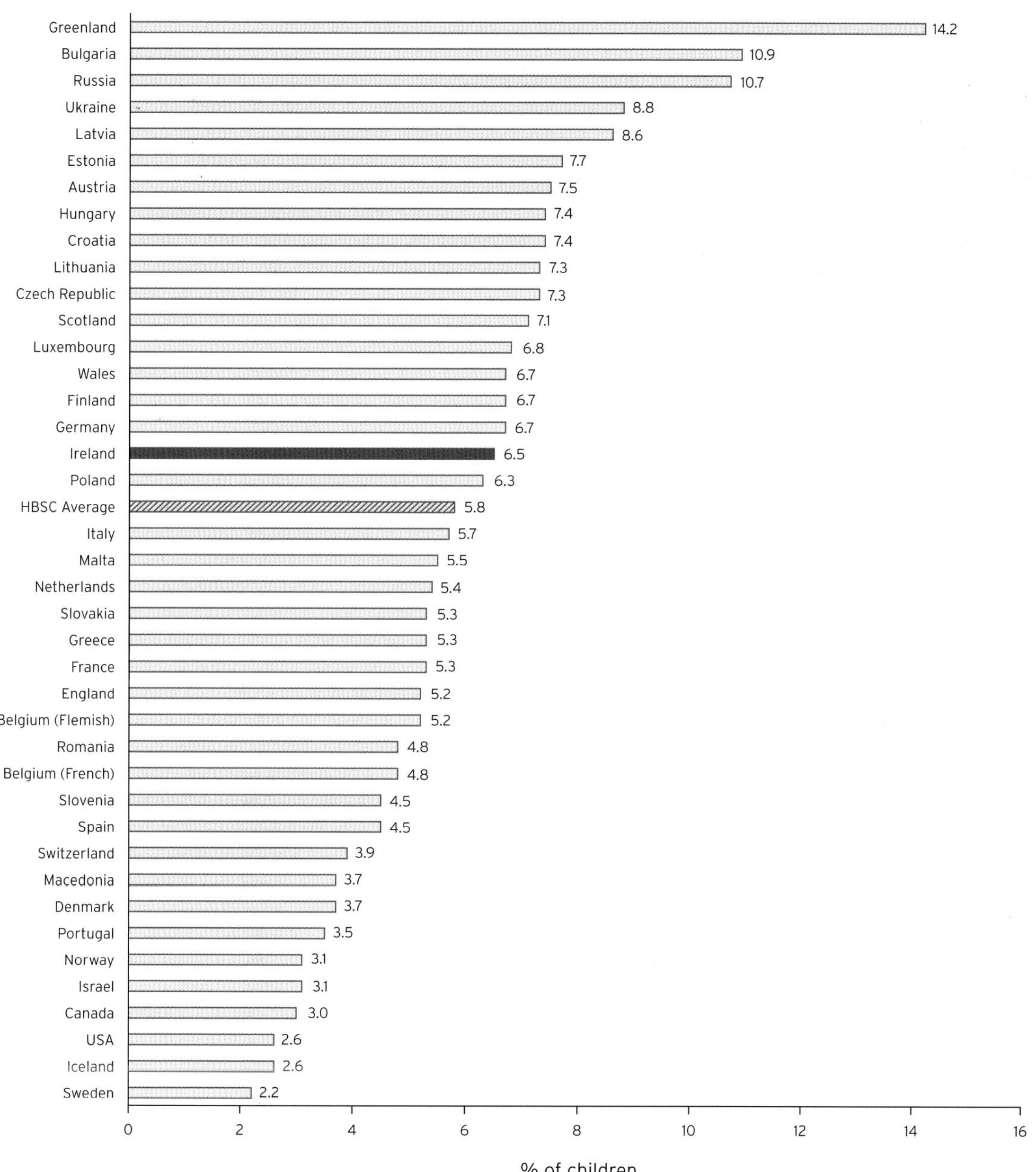

Source: HBSC Survey, Health Promotion Research Centre

ALCOHOL USE

Immigrant children are less likely to report to have been drunk at least once in the last 30 days.

Measure

The percentage of children aged 10-17 who report to have been drunk at least once in the last 30 days.

Key findings

- In 2006, 20.4% of children aged 10-17 reported that they had been drunk at least once in the last 30 days.

Differences by population groups

- When compared to other children, Traveller children were more likely and immigrant children less likely to report being drunk at least once in the last 30 days (*see Table 84*). These differences were statistically significant.
- There were no significant differences between children with and children without a disability and/or chronic illness.

Table 84: Percentage of children who report to have been drunk at least once in the last 30 days, by population groups (2006)

	%
All children	**20.4**
Traveller status	
Traveller children	27.9
All other children	20.5
Immigrant status	
Immigrant children	14.8
All other children	20.7
Disability and/or Chronic Illness status	
Children with a disability and/or chronic illness	20.2
All other children	20.4

Source: HBSC Survey, Health Promotion Research Centre

Differences by age, gender and social class

- Statistically significant differences were also observed across age and gender, with a lower percentage of younger children and a lower percentage of girls reporting to have been drunk at least once in the last 30 days (*see Table 85*).
- The percentage of children in each social class category who reported that they had been drunk at least once in the last 30 days was broadly similar, with no statistical significant differences.

Table 85: Percentage of children who report to have been drunk at least once in the last 30 days, by age, gender and social class (2006)

	Boys (%)	Girls (%)	Total (%)
All children	**21.4**	**19.3**	**20.4**
Age			
10-11	2.7	1.2	1.8
12-14	10.8	9.7	10.3
15-17	38.3	37.7	38.0
Social class			
SC 1-2	20.2	18.5	19.4
SC 3-4	19.5	19.7	19.6
SC 5-6	21.2	18.4	19.8

Source: HBSC Survey, Health Promotion Research Centre

Differences by geographic location

- Children in the Dublin region were more likely to report to have been drunk at least once in the last 30 days (27.4%), while children in the South-West were least likely to report this (13.0%) (*see Table 86*). These differences were statistically significant.

Table 86: Percentage of children who report to have been drunk at least once in the last 30 days, by NUTS Region (2006)

	%
All children	**20.4**
NUTS Region	
Border	17.8
Dublin	27.4
Midlands	26.2
Mid-East	19.3
Mid-West	18.0
South-East	22.0
South-West	13.0
West	19.3

Source: HBSC Survey, Health Promotion Research Centre

International comparisons

- From the 2006 HBSC Survey, using only those in the 15-year-old age group to draw international comparisons, 29.0% of children from Ireland reported that they had been drunk at least once in the last 30 days *(see Figure 18)*. This was significantly higher than the HBSC average of 21.7%.
- Among the 9 countries and regions that used this HBSC item, the lowest percentage for this indicator was found among children from Poland (15.7%) and the highest among children from Austria (30.6%). Overall, children from Ireland ranked 2nd.

Figure 18: Percentage of children aged 15 who report to have been drunk at least once in the last 30 days, by country (2006)

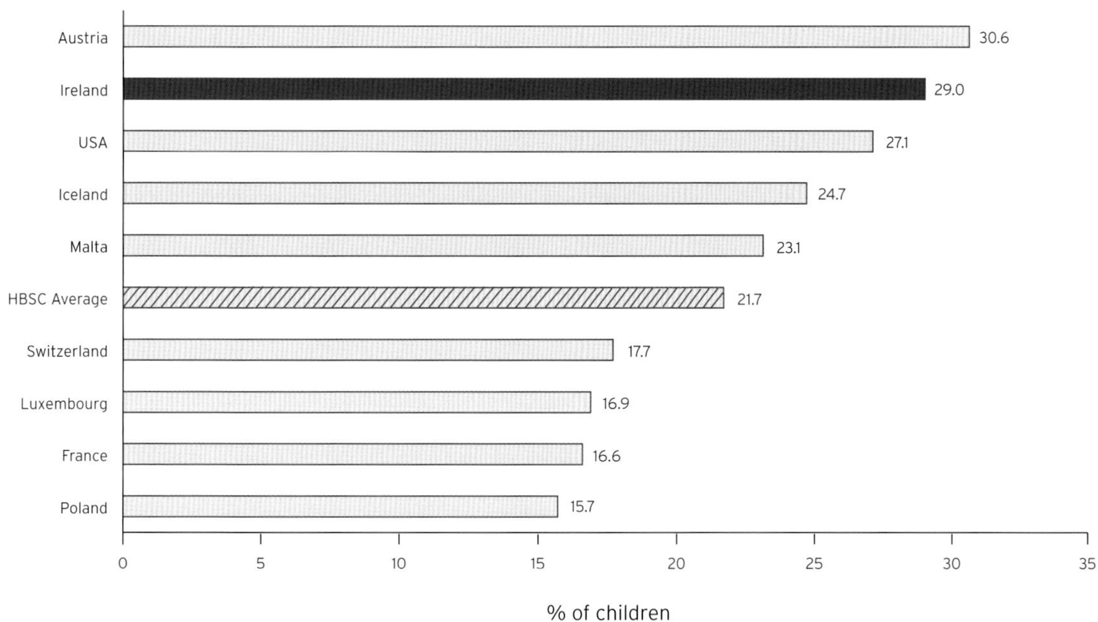

Source: HBSC Survey, Health Promotion Research Centre

CANNABIS USE

Lifetime cannabis use is significantly higher among boys and Traveller children.

Measure

The percentage of children aged 10-17 who report to have taken cannabis at least once in their lifetime.

Key findings

- In 2006, 15.7% of children aged 10-17 reported that they had taken cannabis at least once in their lifetime.

Differences by population groups

- When compared to other children, Traveller children were more likely to report that they had taken cannabis at least once in their lifetime (*see Table 87*). This difference was statistically significant.
- There were no significant differences between immigrant and non-immigrant children or between children with and children without a disability and/or chronic illness.

Table 87: Percentage of children who report to have taken cannabis at least once in their lifetime, by population groups (2006)

	%
All children	**15.7**
Traveller status	
Traveller children	20.7
All other children	15.8
Immigrant status	
Immigrant children	15.5
All other children	15.7
Disability and/or Chronic Illness status	
Children with a disability and/or chronic illness	16.2
All other children	15.6

Source: HBSC Survey, Health Promotion Research Centre

Differences by age, gender, social class and over time

- Statistically significant differences were also observed across age and gender, with a lower percentage of younger children and a lower percentage of girls reporting to have taken cannabis at least once in their lifetime (*see Table 88*).
- The percentage of children in each social class category who reported to have taken cannabis at least once in their lifetime was broadly similar, with no statistical significant differences.

Table 88: Percentage of children who report to have taken cannabis at least once in their lifetime, by age, gender and social class (2002 and 2006)

	2002	2006		
	Total (%)	Boys (%)	Girls (%)	Total (%)
All children	**12.1**	**18.1**	**13.2**	**15.7**
Age				
10-11	0.8	1.5	0.1	0.7
12-14	5.2	10.1	6.4	8.3
15-17	25.9	31.3	26.4	29.0
Social class				
SC 1-2	11.3	16.6	12.1	14.5
SC 3-4	12.2	16.8	13.6	15.2
SC 5-6	13.4	17.5	13.1	15.2

Source: HBSC Survey, Health Promotion Research Centre

Differences by geographic location

- Children in the Dublin region were more likely to report to have taken cannabis at least once in their lifetime (20.3%), while children in the South-West were least likely to report this (11.9%) (*see Table 89*). These differences were statistically significant.

Table 89: Percentage of children who report to have taken cannabis at least once in their lifetime, by NUTS Region (2006)	
	%
All children	**15.7**
NUTS Region	
Border	12.9
Dublin	20.3
Midlands	19.5
Mid-East	16.7
Mid-West	16.1
South-East	15.9
South-West	11.9
West	13.5

Source: HBSC Survey, Health Promotion Research Centre

International comparisons

- From the 2006 HBSC Survey, using only those in the 15-year-old age group to draw international comparisons, 23.5% of children from Ireland reported having ever used cannabis in their lifetime (*see Figure 19*). This was significantly higher than the HBSC average of 18.0%.
- Among all 39 countries and regions that used this HBSC item, the lowest percentage for this indicator was found among children from Romania (3.5%) and the highest among children from Canada (34.5%). Overall, children from Ireland ranked 12th.

Figure 19: Percentage of children aged 15 who report to have taken cannabis at least once in their lifetime, by country (2006)

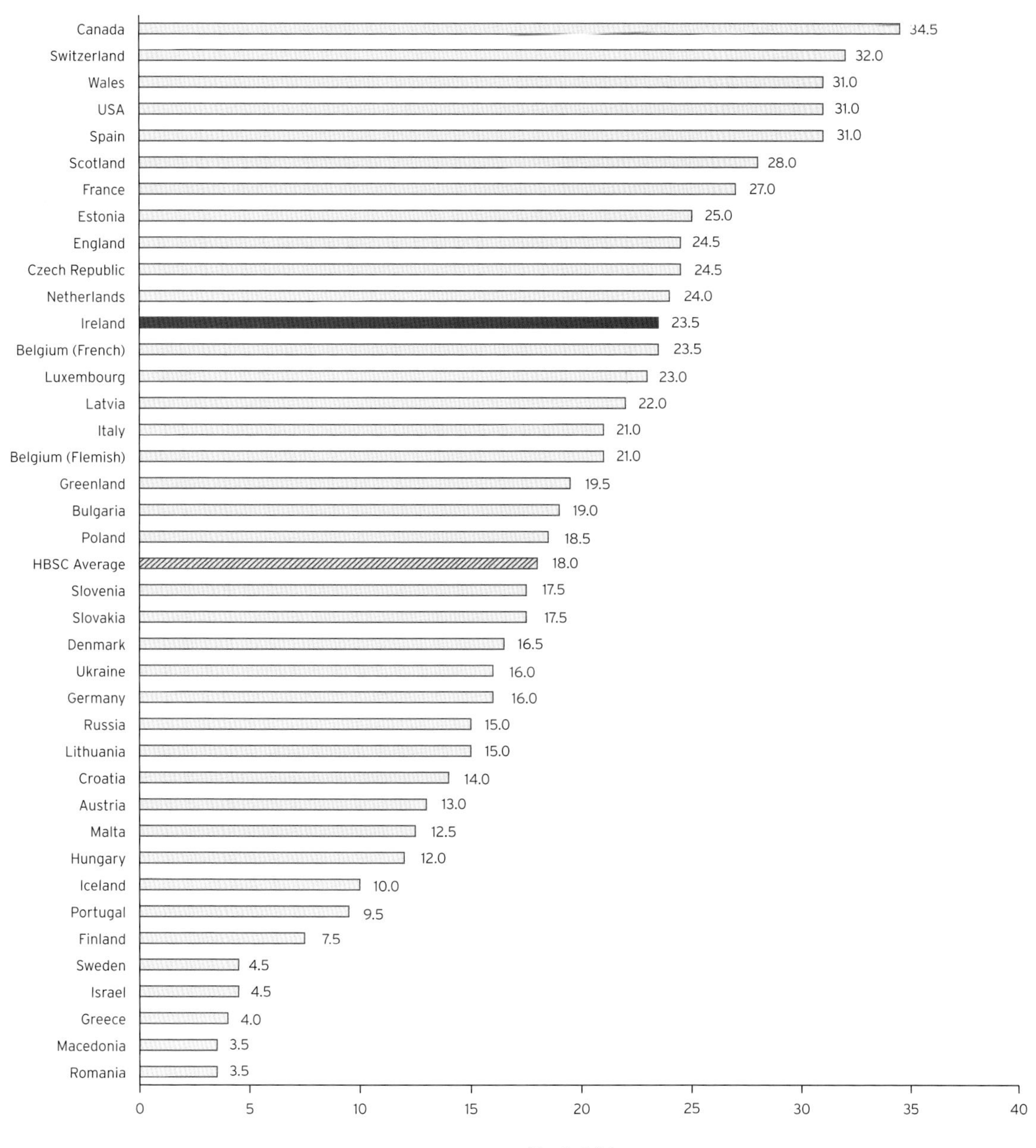

Source: HBSC Survey, Health Promotion Research Centre

SEXUAL HEALTH AND BEHAVIOUR

In 2009, 564 babies were born to teenage girls.

Measure

The number of births to mothers aged 10-17.

Key findings

- In 2009, there were 564 births to mothers aged 10-17 (*see Table 90*).

Table 90: Number and rate (per 100,000) of births, by mothers' age (2005-2009)

	2005		2006		2007		2008		2009	
	No.	Rate	No.	Rate	No.	Rate	No.	Rate	No.	Rate
Total (all ages)	**61,372**	**5,659**	**65,425**	**5,882**	**71,389**	**6,245**	**75,065**	**6,461**	**74,278**	**6,398**
Age										
15-17*	612	724	564	674	624	736	610	724	564	684
18-24	9,547	4,189	10,169	4,459	10,800	4,724	11,108	4,971	10,392	4,938
25+	51,127	6,622	54,660	6,827	59,946	7,224	63,323	7,413	63,289	7,291
Not stated	86	–	32	–	19	–	24	–	33	–

* The number of births to mothers aged 15-17 includes a small number to mothers aged 10-14 years. There were 5 babies born to mothers in the 10-14 age group in 2009.

Source: Vital Statistics and Census Population Estimates, CSO

Differences over time

- Over the period 2005-2009, the number of births to mothers aged 10-17 has decreased, from 612 in 2005 to 564 in 2009 (*see Figure 20*).

Figure 20: Number of births to mothers aged 10-17 (2005-2009)

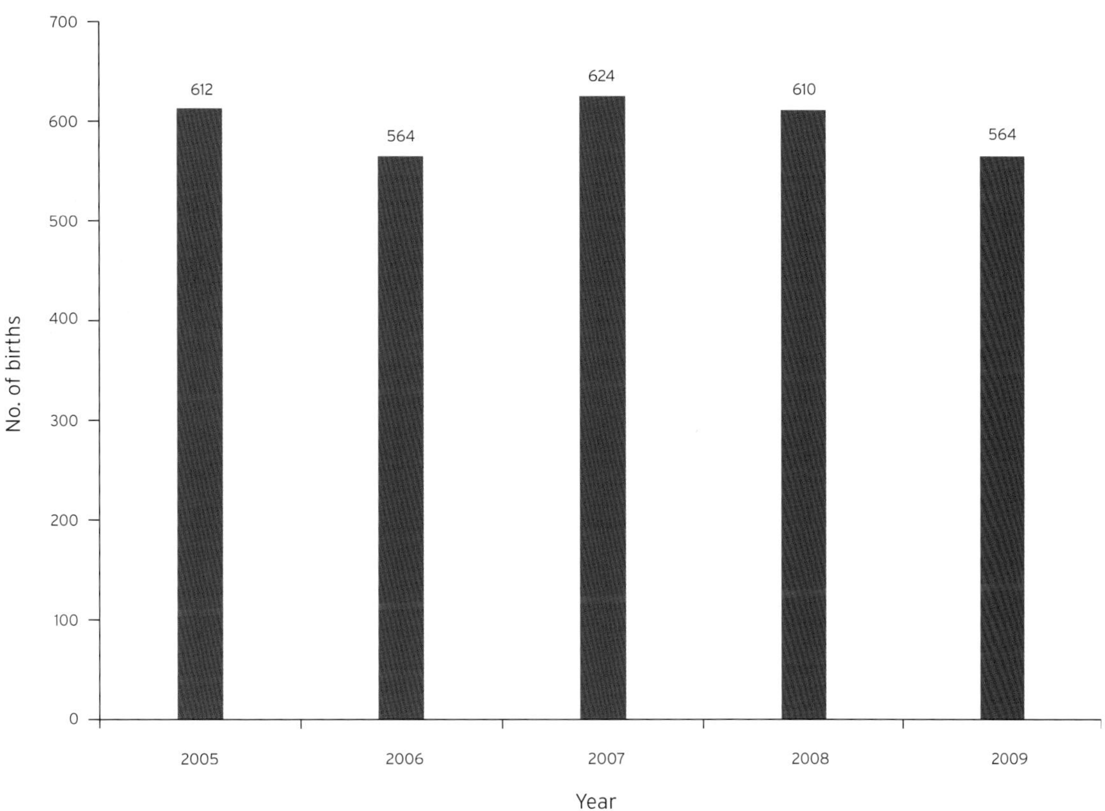

Source: Vital Statistics and Census Population Estimates, CSO

Differences by geographic location

- Louth had the highest proportion of births to mothers aged 10-17 (*see Table 91*).

Table 91: Number and percentage of births to mothers aged 10-17, by county (2009)

	No. of births to 10-17 year-olds	No. of births to all ages	Births to 10-17 year-olds as % of all births
State	**564**	**74,278**	**0.8**
County			
Carlow	12	976	1.2
Clare	12	1,889	0.6
Cork	39	8,477	0.5
Donegal	27	2,284	1.2
Dublin	195	20,607	0.9
Galway	18	3,974	0.5
Kildare	29	3,942	0.7
Kilkenny	12	1,392	0.9
Laois	16	1,368	1.2
Limerick	29	3,121	0.9
Louth	27	1,858	1.5
Mayo	11	1,854	0.6
Meath	19	3,474	0.5
Monaghan	4	790	0.5
Offaly	5	1,229	0.4
Sligo	6	944	0.6
Tipperary	16	2,552	0.6
Waterford	12	1,878	0.6
Westmeath	11	1,390	0.8
Wexford	23	2,385	1.0
Wicklow	12	2,435	0.5
Other counties	29	5,459	0.5

Source: Vital Statistics, CSO

SELF-ESTEEM

Approximately 4 in 10 girls aged 15-17 report feeling happy with the way they are.

Measure

The percentage of children aged 9-17 who report feeling happy with the way they are.

Key findings

- In 2006, 58.2% of children aged 9-17 reported feeling happy with the way they are.

Differences by population groups

- When compared to other children, immigrant children and children with a disability and/or chronic illness were less likely to report feeling happy with the way they are (*see Table 92*). These differences were statistically significant.
- There were no significant differences between Traveller and non-Traveller children.

Table 92: Percentage of children who report feeling happy with the way they are, by population groups (2006)

	%
All children	**58.2**
Traveller status	
Traveller children	56.6
All other children	58.1
Immigrant status	
Immigrant children	53.7
All other children	58.4
Disability and/or Chronic Illness status	
Children with a disability and/or chronic illness	54.2
All other children	59.1

Source: HBSC Survey, Health Promotion Research Centre

Differences by age, gender and social class

- Statistically significant differences were also observed across age and gender, with a lower percentage of older children and a lower percentage of girls reporting to feel happy with the way they are (*see Table 93*).
- The percentage of children in each social class category who reported feeling happy with the way they are was broadly similar, with no statistical significant differences.

Table 93: Percentage of children who report feeling happy with the way they are, by age, gender and social class (2006)

	Boys (%)	Girls (%)	Total (%)
All children	**62.9**	**53.1**	**58.2**
Age			
9	77.8	78.8	78.3
10-11	74.6	74.5	74.6
12-14	65.3	56.4	61.1
15-17	57.4	40.2	49.3
Social class			
SC 1-2	63.1	51.8	57.2
SC 3-4	63.2	53.1	58.2
SC 5-6	63.6	55.2	59.2

Source: HBSC Survey, Health Promotion Research Centre

Differences by geographic location

- Children in the South-West region were more likely to report feeling happy with the way they are (61.3%), while children in the Mid-West were least likely to report this (54.0%) (*see Table 94*). These differences were statistically significant.

Table 94: Percentage of children who report feeling happy with the way they are, by NUTS Region (2006)	
	%
All children	**58.2**
NUTS Region	
Border	60.0
Dublin	58.0
Midlands	57.1
Mid-East	58.0
Mid-West	54.0
South-East	58.3
South-West	61.3
West	55.4

Source: HBSC Survey, Health Promotion Research Centre

SELF-REPORTED HAPPINESS

Self-reported happiness levels are significantly lower among Traveller children, immigrant children and children with a disability and/or chronic illness.

Measure

The percentage of children aged 9-17 who report being happy with their lives at present.

Key findings

- In 2006, 90.8% of children aged 9-17 reported being happy with their lives at present.

Differences by population groups

- The percentages of Traveller children, immigrant children and children with a disability and/or chronic illness who reported being happy with their lives at present were significantly lower than the corresponding percentages of non-Traveller children, non-immigrant children and children without a disability and/or chronic illness (*see Table 95*).

Table 95: Percentage of children who report being happy with their lives at present, by population groups (2006)

	%
All children	**90.8**
Traveller status	
Traveller children	86.1
All other children	90.9
Immigrant status	
Immigrant children	87.3
All other children	91.0
Disability and/or Chronic Illness status	
Children with a disability and/or chronic illness	87.6
All other children	91.6

Source: HBSC Survey, Health Promotion Research Centre

Differences by age, gender, social class and over time

- Statistically significant differences were also observed across age and gender, with a lower percentage of older children and a lower percentage of girls reporting to be happy with their lives at present (*see Table 96*).
- The percentage of children in each social class category who reported being happy with their lives at present was broadly similar, with no statistical significant differences.

Table 96: Percentage of children who report being happy with their lives at present, by age, gender and social class (1998, 2002 and 2006)

	1998	2002	2006		
	Total (%)	Total (%)	Boys (%)	Girls (%)	Total (%)
All children	**88.6**	**89.5**	**92.4**	**89.1**	**90.8**
Age					
9	–	–	95.0	96.0	95.5
10-11	93.3	94.8	95.0	95.6	95.4
12-14	89.6	90.1	92.6	90.4	91.5
15-17	84.0	86.5	91.7	85.0	88.5
Social class					
SC 1-2	87.3	91.4	94.2	89.2	91.8
SC 3-4	89.3	90.1	93.0	89.7	91.4
SC 5-6	89.8	89.9	91.4	90.7	91.0

Source: HBSC Survey, Health Promotion Research Centre

Differences by geographic location

- Children in the South-East region were more likely to report being happy with their lives at present (92.2%), while children in the Midlands were least likely to report this (87.4%) *(see Table 97)*. These differences were statistically significant.

Table 97: Percentage of children who report being happy with their lives at present, by NUTS Region (2006)

	%
All children	**90.8**
NUTS Region	
Border	91.9
Dublin	90.2
Midlands	87.4
Mid-East	90.6
Mid-West	91.5
South-East	92.2
South-West	91.2
West	89.7

Source: HBSC Survey, Health Promotion Research Centre

YOUTH SUICIDE

In 2009, 21 young children took their own lives.

Measure

The number of suicides of children aged 10-17.

Key findings

- In 2009, there were 21 suicides of children aged 10-17.

Differences by gender and over time

- The number and rate (per 100,000) of suicides was higher among boys (*see Table 98*).
- Over the period 2005-2009, the rate of suicides of boys has risen slightly, from 14 per 100,000 in 2005 to 15 per 100,000 in 2009. Over the same period, the rate of suicides of girls aged 15-17 has doubled, from 5 per 100,000 in 2005 to 10 per 100,000 in 2009.

Table 98: Number and rate (per 100,000) of suicides, by age and gender (2005-2009)

Year	15-17 years				18-24 years				All ages	
	Boys		Girls		Men		Women		Total	
	No.	Rate	No.	Rate	No.	Rate	No.	Rate	No.	Rate
2005	12	14	4	5	72	31	17	7	481	12
2006	14	16	4	5	77	33	14	6	460	11
2007	11	12	5	6	72	31	11	5	458	11
2008	16	18	8	10	63	28	13	6	424	10
2009	13	15	8	10	60	29	13	6	527	12

Source: Vital Statistics, CSO

- Overall, suicide accounted for 23.1% of all deaths of children aged 10-17 (*see Table 99*).

Table 99: Suicides as a percentage of total deaths of children aged 10-17, by gender (2005-2009)

	2005	2006	2007	2008	2009
Total	**15.5**	**17.7**	**14.3**	**23.8**	**23.1**
Gender					
Boys	17.9	23.2	14.5	21.9	21.7
Girls	11.1	10.0	13.9	28.6	25.8

Source: Vital Statistics, CSO

PHYSICAL ACTIVITY

Children in Ireland have the highest levels of physical activity among 41 OECD countries.

Measure

The percentage of children aged 9-17 who report being physically active for at least 60 minutes per day on more than 4 days per week.

Key findings

- In 2006, 54.8% of children aged 9-17 reported being physically active for at least 60 minutes per day for more than 4 days per week.

Differences by population groups

- When compared to other children, immigrant children were less likely to report being physically active for at least 60 minutes per day on more than 4 days per week (*see Table 100*). This difference was statistically significant.
- There were no significant differences between Traveller and non-Traveller children or between children with and children without a disability and/or chronic illness.

Table 100: Percentage of children who report being physically active for at least 60 minutes per day on more than 4 days per week, by population groups (2006)

	%
All children	**54.8**
Traveller status	
Traveller children	56.5
All other children	54.6
Immigrant status	
Immigrant children	50.1
All other children	55.1
Disability and/or Chronic Illness status	
Children with a disability and/or chronic illness	54.9
All other children	54.7

Source: HBSC Survey, Health Promotion Research Centre

Differences by age, gender, social class and over time

- Statistically significant differences were also observed across age and gender, with a lower percentage of older children and a lower percentage of girls reporting being physically active for at least 60 minutes per day on more than 4 days per week (*see Table 101*).
- The percentage of children in each social class category who reported being physically active for at least 60 minutes per day on more than 4 days per week was broadly similar, with no statistical significant differences.

Table 101: Percentage of children who report being physically active for at least 60 minutes per day on more than 4 days per week, by age, gender and social class (2002 and 2006)

	2002	2006		
	Total (%)	Boys (%)	Girls (%)	Total (%)
All children	**47.4**	**63.4**	**45.9**	**54.8**
Age				
9	–	80.6	78.4	79.5
10-11	59.8	80.8	71.0	75.1
12-14	51.1	69.6	52.6	61.5
15-17	37.7	51.6	26.8	39.9
Social class				
SC 1-2	48.6	63.7	46.1	55.2
SC 3-4	48.0	64.1	44.1	54.3
SC 5-6	46.1	63.7	47.6	55.3

Source: HBSC Survey, Health Promotion Research Centre

Differences by geographic location

- Children in the Mid-East region were more likely to report being physically active for at least 60 minutes per day on more than 4 days per week (58.4%), while children in the Border region were least likely to report this (50.4%) (*see Table 102*). These differences were statistically significant.

Table 102: Percentage of children who report being physically active for at least 60 minutes per day on more than 4 days per week, by NUTS Region (2006)	
	%
All children	**54.8**
NUTS Region	
Border	50.4
Dublin	56.1
Midlands	53.5
Mid-East	58.4
Mid-West	52.6
South-East	58.0
South-West	53.9
West	50.7

Source: HBSC Survey, Health Promotion Research Centre

International comparisons

- From the 2006 HBSC Survey, using the ages of 11, 13 and 15 only to draw international comparisons, 59.2% of children from Ireland reported being physically active for at least 60 minutes per day on more than 4 days per week (*see Figure 21*). This was significantly higher than the HBSC average of 42.6%.
- Among all 41 countries and regions that used this HBSC item, the lowest percentage for this indicator was found among children from Russia (28.6%) and the highest among children from Ireland (59.2%). Overall, children from Ireland ranked 1st.

Figure 21: Percentage of children who report being physically active for at least 60 minutes per day on more than 4 days per week, by country (2006)

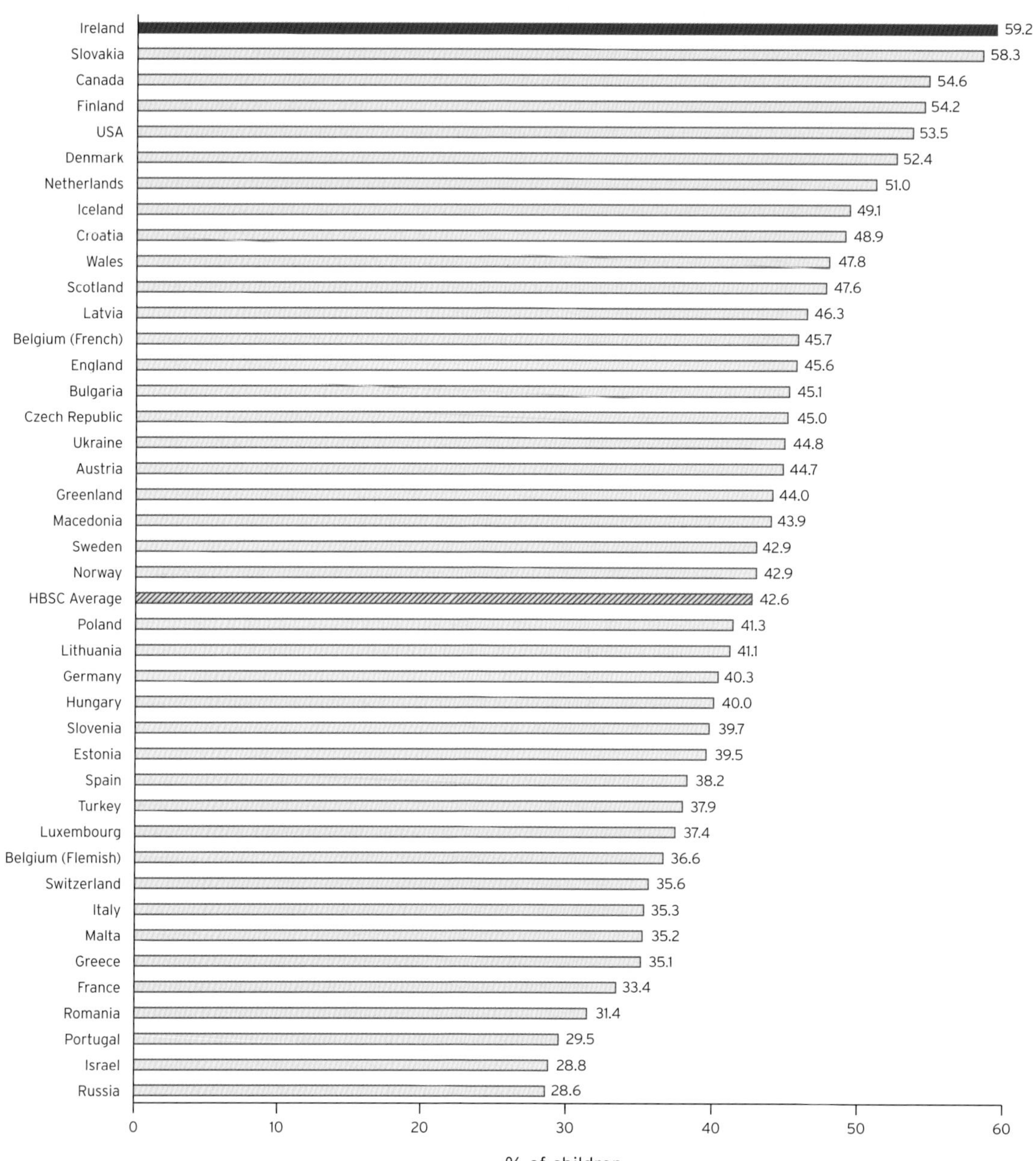

Source: HBSC Survey, Health Promotion Research Centre

EATING HABITS

Boys and younger children are more likely to eat breakfast on 5 or more days per week.

Measure

The percentage of children aged 9-17 who report eating breakfast on 5 or more days per week.

Key findings

- In 2006, 76.0% of children aged 9-17 reported eating breakfast on 5 or more days per week.

Differences by population groups

- The percentages of Traveller children, immigrant children and children with a disability and/or chronic illness who reported eating breakfast on 5 or more days per week were significantly lower than the corresponding percentages of non-Traveller children, non-immigrant children and children without a disability and/or chronic illness (*see Table 103*).

Table 103: Percentage of children who report to eat breakfast on 5 or more days per week, by population groups (2006)

	%
All children	**76.0**
Traveller status	
Traveller children	64.7
All other children	77.3
Immigrant status	
Immigrant children	71.7
All other children	77.4
Disability and/or Chronic Illness status	
Children with a disability and/or chronic illness	74.8
All other children	77.7

Source: HBSC Survey, Health Promotion Research Centre

Differences by age, gender, social class and over time

- Statistically significant differences were also observed across age, gender and social class categories, with a higher percentage of boys, younger children and children in the higher social class category reporting to eat breakfast on 5 days or more per week (*see Table 104*).

Table 104: Percentage of children who report to eat breakfast on 5 or more days per week, by age, gender and social class (2002 and 2006)

	2002	2006		
	Total (%)	Boys (%)	Girls (%)	Total (%)
All children	**77.3**	**79.1**	**72.9**	**76.0**
Age				
9	–	85.6	88.3	87.0
10-11	87.4	83.4	83.0	83.2
12-14	78.9	81.8	75.2	78.6
15-17	70.9	75.2	66.3	71.0
Social class				
SC 1-2	81.5	83.2	78.4	80.9
SC 3-4	75.3	79.7	71.1	75.7
SC 5-6	77.7	77.6	71.7	74.5

Source: HBSC Survey, Health Promotion Research Centre

Differences by geographic location

- Children in the West region were more likely to report eating breakfast on 5 or more days per week (78.8%), while children in the Midlands were least likely to report this (70.1%) (*see Table 105*). These differences were statistically significant.

Table 105: Percentage of children who report to eat breakfast on 5 or more days per week, by NUTS Region (2006)	
	%
All children	**76.0**
NUTS Region	
Border	77.7
Dublin	73.5
Midlands	70.1
Mid-East	74.6
Mid-West	77.5
South-East	76.0
South-West	77.2
West	78.8

Source: HBSC Survey, Health Promotion Research Centre

International comparisons

- From the 2006 HBSC Survey, using the ages of 11, 13 and 15 only to draw international comparisons, 78.2% of children from Ireland reported eating breakfast on 5 or more days per week (*see Figure 22*). This was significantly higher than the HBSC average of 72.2%.
- Among all 39 countries and regions that used this HBSC item, the lowest percentage for this indicator was found among Greek children (51.5%) and the highest among children from Portugal (87.8%). Overall, children from Ireland ranked 10th.

Figure 22: Percentage of children who report to eat breakfast on 5 or more days per week, by country (2006)

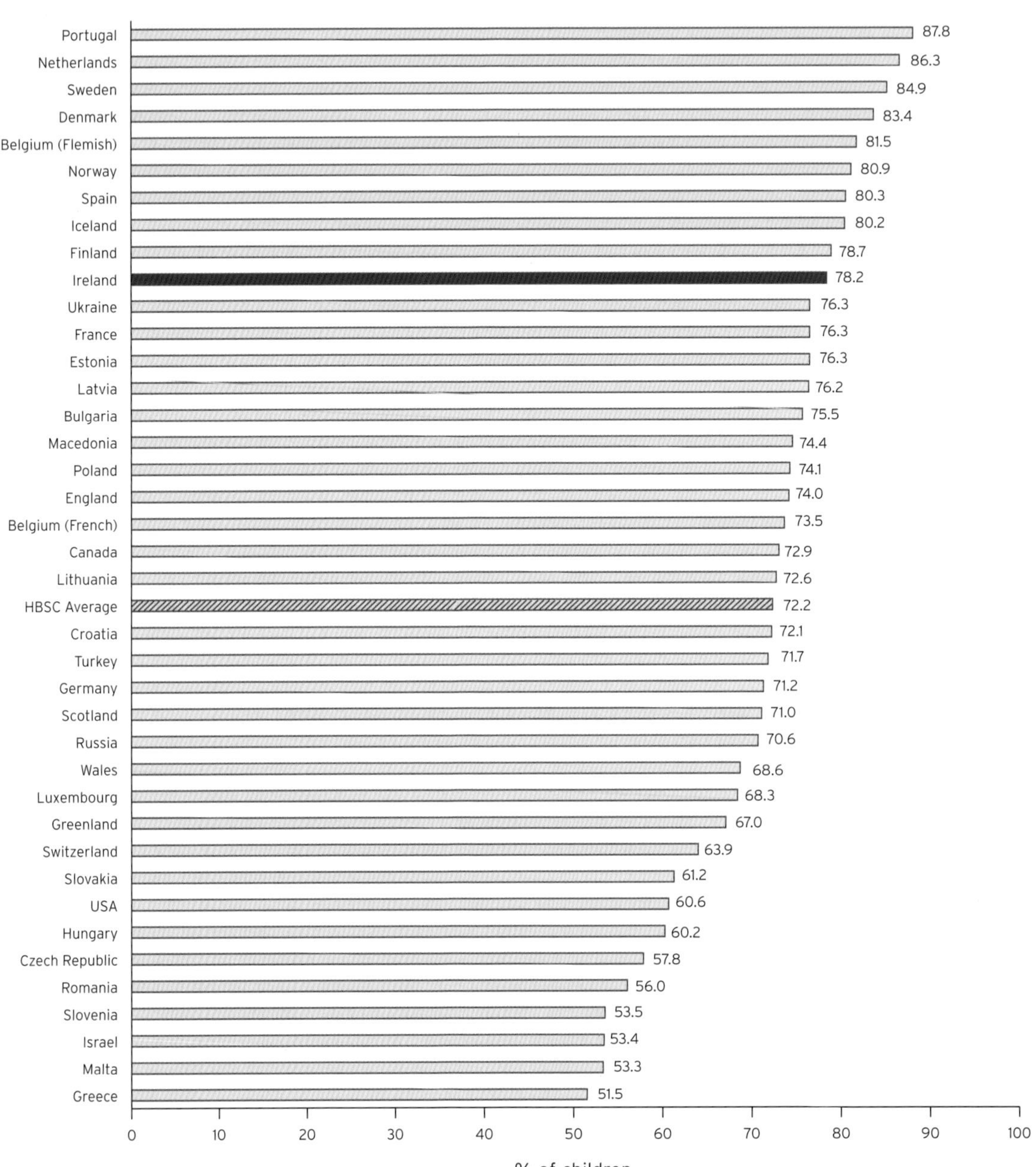

Source: HBSC Survey, Health Promotion Research Centre

PART 4:
FORMAL AND INFORMAL SUPPORTS

PUBLIC EXPENDITURE ON EDUCATION

Since 2002, Ireland's expenditure on education has increased.

Measure

Public expenditure on education

Key findings

- In 2007, public expenditure on education in Ireland represented 5.7% of Gross National Income (GNI), higher than the EU-27 average of 5% of Gross Domestic Product (GDP).

Differences over time

- Public expenditure on education in Ireland decreased from 4.8% of GDP in 1998 to 4.3% of GDP in 2002, before rising to 4.9% in 2007 (*see Figure 23*).

Figure 23: Public expenditure on education in Ireland and in EU-27 (1998-2007)

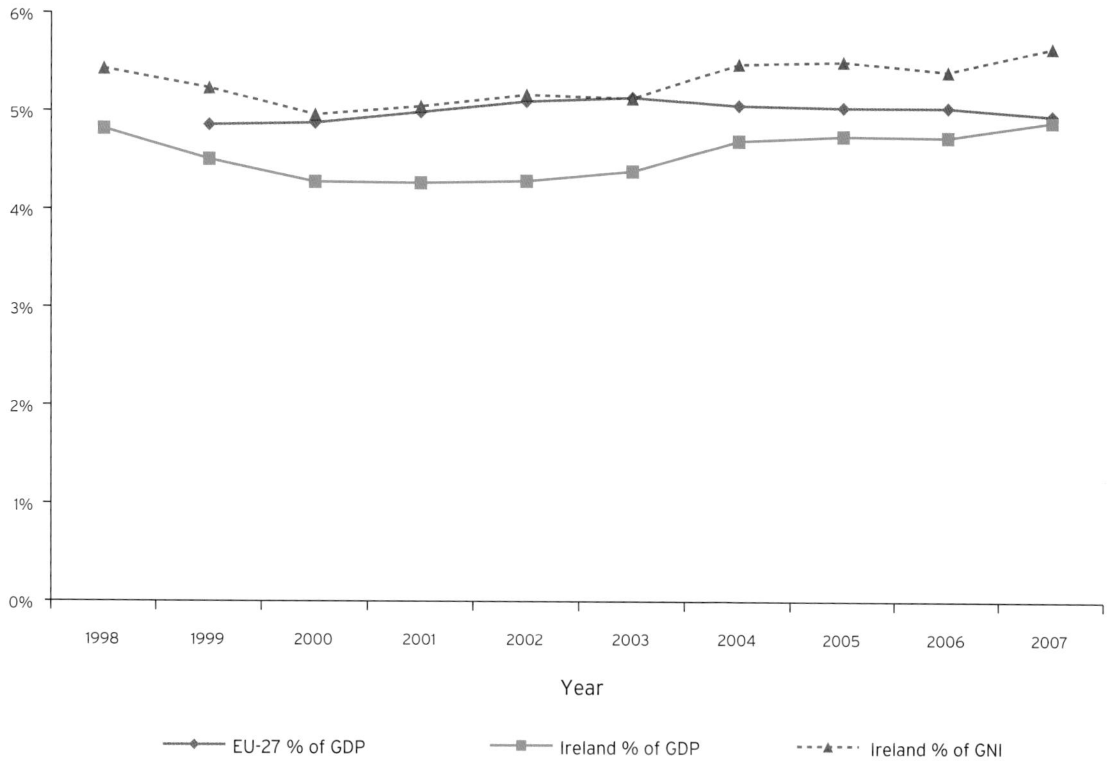

Source: Department of Education and Skills; Eurostat

Differences by geographic location

- In 2006, expenditure on education in Ireland as a percentage of GDP was 4.7%, just below the EU average of 5% (*see Table 106*). However, when expressed as a percentage of GNI, the figure for Ireland rises to 5.4%.

Table 106: Public expenditure on education as % of GDP in EU-27 (2004-2006)			
	2004	**2005**	**2006**
EU-27	**5.1**	**5.0**	**5.0**
Country			
Austria	5.5	5.5	5.4
Belgium	6.0	6.0	6.0
Bulgaria	4.5	4.5	4.2
Cyprus	6.7	6.9	7.0
Czech Republic	4.4	4.3	4.6
Denmark	8.4	8.3	8.0
Estonia	4.9	4.9	4.8
Finland	6.4	6.3	6.1
France	5.8	5.7	5.6
Germany	4.6	4.5	4.4
Greece	3.8	4.0	*n/a*
Hungary	5.4	5.5	5.4
Ireland (% of GDP)	**4.7**	**4.8**	**4.7**
Ireland (% of GNI)	**5.5**	**5.5**	**5.4**
Italy	4.6	4.4	4.7
Latvia	5.1	5.1	5.1
Lithuania	5.2	4.9	4.8
Luxembourg	3.9	3.8	3.4
Malta	4.8	6.8	*n/a*
Netherlands	5.5	5.5	5.5
Poland	5.4	5.5	5.3
Portugal	5.3	5.4	5.3
Romania	3.3	3.5	*n/a*
Slovakia	4.2	3.9	3.8
Slovenia	5.8	5.7	5.7
Spain	4.3	4.2	4.3
Sweden	7.2	7.0	6.9
United Kingdom	5.2	5.4	5.5

n/a = not available
Source: Department of Education and Skills; Eurostat

- Real non-capital public expenditure per student in Ireland increased by 58.3% for first-level and by 55.7% for second-level over the period 1999-2008, when measured in constant 2008 prices (*see Table 107*). The corresponding increase in expenditure on third-level over the same period was 2.5 % in constant prices.

Table 107: Real non-capital public expenditure on education, by educational level (1999-2008)

Year	Expenditure per pupil at 2008 prices (€) Educational level			€m (at 2008 prices)
	First	Second[1]	Third[2]	Total non-capital expenditure
1999	4,136	6,069	11,288	5,473
2000	4,449	6,372	10,964	5,698
2001	4,613	6,985	11,412	6,020
2002	5,064	7,453	11,456	6,425
2003	5,532	8,000	11,257	6,847
2004	5,944	8,070	10,909	7,051
2005	6,060	8,397	11,316	7,274
2006	6,293	8,803	11,848	7,640
2007	6,442	9,268	11,673	7,967
2008	6,546	9,447	11,567	8,211

[1] Includes Further Education sector (i.e. Post-Leaving Certificate courses).

[2] Based on full-time equivalents.

Source: Department of Education and Skills

AT RISK OF POVERTY

Children in the Midlands region are three times more likely to be at risk of poverty than children in the Dublin region.

Measure

The percentage of children living in households with an equivalised household disposable income below the 60% median.

Key findings

- In 2009, 18.6% of children under 18 were considered to be at risk of poverty (*see Table 108*).
- Children under 18 had a higher risk of being poor than the population as a whole (18.6% compared to 14.1%).

Table 108: Percentage of persons at risk of poverty (2005-2009)

	2005	2006	2007	2008	2009
Children under 18	23.1	22.3	19.9	18.0	18.6
All persons	18.5	17.0	16.5	14.4	14.1

Source: EU-SILC, CSO

Differences over time

- The percentage of children under 18 considered to be at risk of poverty fell from 23.1% in 2005 to 18.6% in 2009.

Differences by geographic location

- The percentage of children under 18 considered to be at risk of poverty was lowest in the Dublin region (10.8%) and highest in the Midlands region (31.0%) (*see Figure 24*).

International comparisons

- In 2008, 18.3% of children under 18 were at risk of poverty in Ireland. This was lower than the EU-27 average of 20.3% (*see Figure 24*).

Figure 24: Percentage of children under 18 at risk of poverty by EU-27 (2008) and percentage of children under 18 at risk of poverty by NUTS Region (2009)

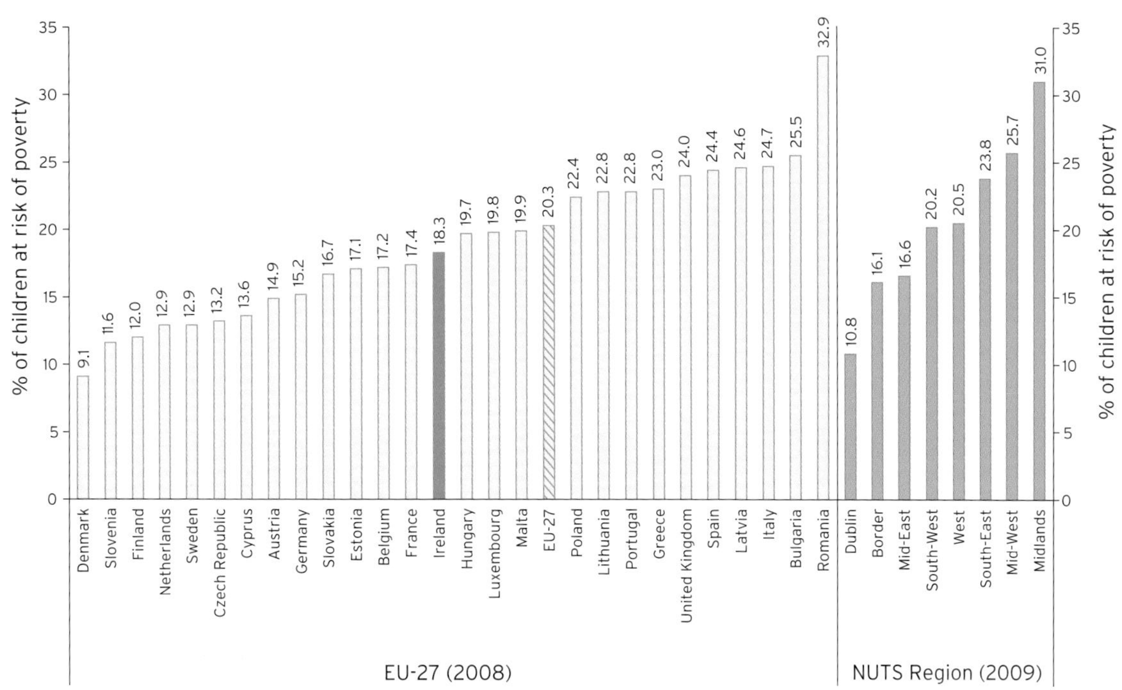

Source: Eurostat

CONSISTENT POVERTY

The percentage of children in the South-East region experiencing consistent poverty is approximately twice as high as the national average.

Measure

The percentage of children living in households with an equivalised household disposable income below the 60% median who experienced at least two forms of enforced deprivation.

Key findings

- In 2009, 8.7% of children under 18 experienced consistent poverty (*see Table 109*).
- Children under 18 were more likely to experience consistent poverty than the population as a whole (8.7% compared to 5.5%).

Table 109: Percentage of persons experiencing consistent poverty (2005-2009)

	2005	2006	2007	2008	2009
Children under 18	10.7	11.0	7.4	6.3	8.7
All persons	7.0	6.9	5.1	4.2	5.5

Source: EU-SILC, CSO

Differences by household structure and over time

- The percentage of children under 18 experiencing consistent poverty fell from 11.0% in 2006 to 6.3% in 2008. This percentage increased significantly to 8.7% in 2009 (*see Table 109*).
- The consistent poverty rate of persons living in households comprising a single adult with children was 16.6% (*see Figure 25*). This was substantially higher than the consistent poverty rate in households with 2 adults and 1-3 children (5.4%) and other households with children under 18 years (6.3%).

Differences by geographic location

- The percentage of children under 18 experiencing consistent poverty was lowest in the Mid-East region (4.1%) and highest in the South-East region (18.5%) (*see Figure 25*).

Figure 25: Percentage of persons experiencing consistent poverty by household structure (2009) and percentage of children experiencing consistent poverty by NUTS Region (2009)

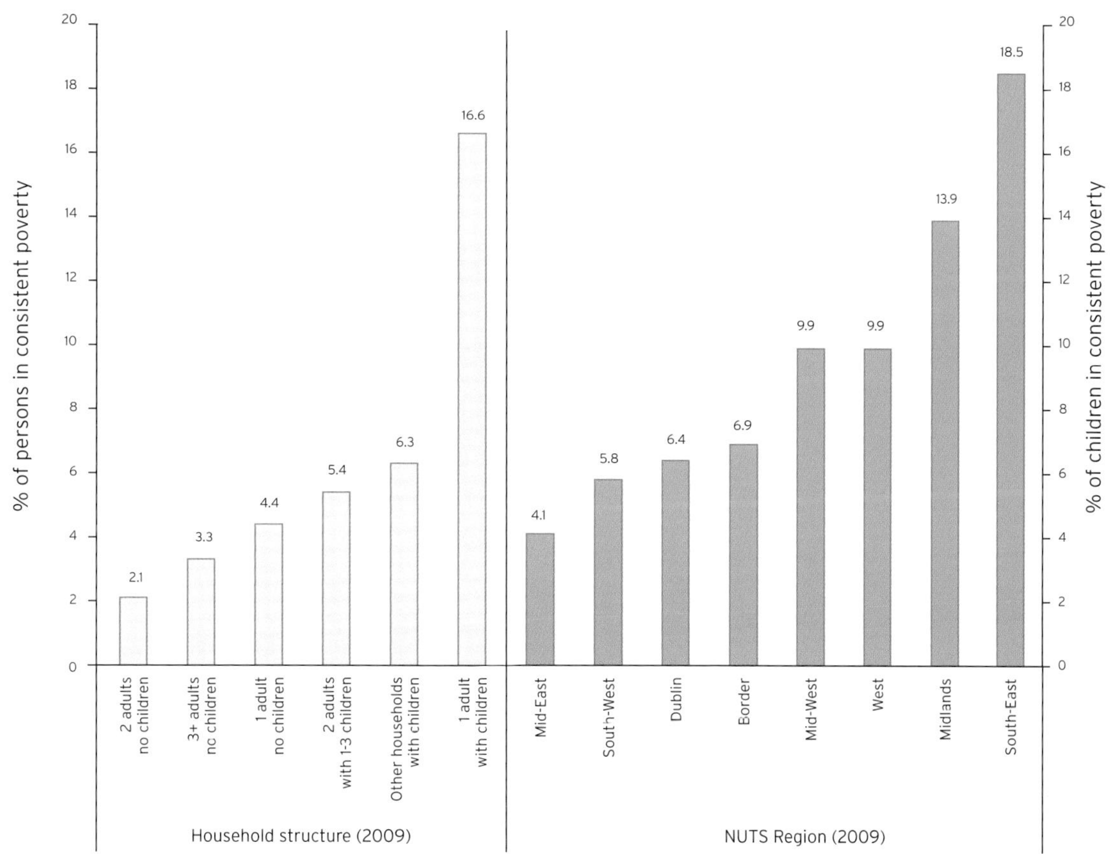

Source: EU-SILC, CSO

AVAILABILITY OF HOUSING FOR FAMILIES WITH CHILDREN

The number of households with children in need of social housing has increased by 24% since 2005.

Measure

The number of households with children identified as being in need of social housing.

Key findings

- In 2008, there were 27,704 households with children identified as being in need of social housing.

Differences by household structure and over time

- 55.5% (15,369) of households with children identified as being in need of social housing were households with one child; 27.0% (7,479) were households with 2 children; 10.5% (2,924) were households with 3 children; and the remaining 7.0% (1,932) of households included 4 or more children *(see Table 110)*.
- The number of households with children identified as being in need of social housing has increased by 24% since 2005.

Table 110: Number and percentage of households with children identified as being in need of social housing, by number of children (selected years 1996-2008)

	1996	1999	2002	2005	2008	
	No.	No.	No.	No.	No.	%
Total	**17,773**	**25,185**	**29,484**	**22,335**	**27,704**	**100.0**
No. of children						
1	10,816	14,734	17,523	13,703	15,369	55.5
2	4,112	6,117	7,250	5,385	7,479	27.0
3	1,559	2,402	2,685	1,991	2,924	10.5
4	690	1,036	1,126	772	1,210	4.4
5 or more	596	896	900	484	722	2.6

Source: Triennial Assessment of Housing Needs, Department of the Environment, Heritage and Local Government

Differences by household structure and geographic location

- 29.4% (8,135) of households with children identified as being in need of social housing were in Dublin (*see Table 111*).
- 72.4% (20,059) of households with children identified as being in need of social housing were one-parent households and the remaining 27.6% (7,645) were two-parent households.

Table 111: Number and percentage of households with children identified as being in need of social housing, by household structure and county (2008)

	Single with child/children	Couple with child/children	All households with child/children	
	No.	No.	No.	%
Total	**20,059**	**7,645**	**27,704**	**100.0**
County				
Carlow	299	167	466	1.7
Cavan	184	98	282	1.0
Clare	428	280	708	2.6
Cork	1,867	818	2,685	9.7
Donegal	917	217	1,134	4.1
Dublin	6,132	2,003	8,135	29.4
Galway	1,079	481	1,560	5.6
Kerry	663	248	911	3.3
Kildare	1,196	443	1,639	5.9
Kilkenny	299	123	422	1.5
Laois	180	90	270	1.0
Leitrim	71	54	125	0.5
Limerick	865	291	1,156	4.2
Longford	137	115	252	0.9
Louth	591	353	944	3.4
Mayo	453	182	635	2.3
Meath	612	239	851	3.1
Monaghan	189	101	290	1.0
Offaly	404	185	589	2.1
Roscommon	189	77	266	1.0
Sligo	160	72	232	0.8
Tipperary NR	216	109	325	1.2
Tipperary SR	306	96	402	1.5
Waterford	558	143	701	2.5
Westmeath	302	102	404	1.5
Wexford	853	296	1,149	4.1
Wicklow	909	262	1,171	4.2

Source: Triennial Assessment of Housing Needs, Department of the Environment, Heritage and Local Government

COMMUNITY CHARACTERISTICS

Traveller children and children with a disability and/or chronic illness are less likely to report feeling safe in the area where they live.

Measure

The percentage of children aged 9-17 who report feeling safe in the area where they live.

Key findings

- In 2006, 90.4% of children aged 9-17 reported feeling safe in the area where they live.

Differences by population groups

- When compared to other children, Traveller children and children with a disability and/or chronic illness were less likely to report feeling safe in the area where they live (*see Table 112*). These differences were statistically significant.
- There were no significant differences between immigrant and non-immigrant children.

Table 112: Percentage of children who report feeling safe in area where they live, by population groups (2006)

	%
All children	**90.4**
Traveller status	
Traveller children	77.5
All other children	90.7
Immigrant status	
Immigrant children	89.8
All other children	90.4
Disability and/or Chronic Illness status	
Children with a disability and/or chronic illness	87.1
All other children	91.2

Source: HBSC Survey, Health Promotion Research Centre

Differences by age, gender, social class and over time

- The percentage of children who reported feeling safe in the area where they live was broadly similar across age and gender, with no statistically significant differences (*see Table 113*).
- Statistically significant differences were observed across social class, with a lower percentage of children from the lowest social category reporting to feel safe in the area where they live.

Table 113: Percentage of children who report feeling safe in area where they live, by age, gender and social class (2002 and 2006)

	2002	2006		
	Total (%)	Boys (%)	Girls (%)	Total (%)
All children	**87.4**	**90.4**	**90.4**	**90.4**
Age				
9	–	90.5	89.8	90.2
10-11	87.4	90.0	89.8	89.9
12-14	87.6	90.6	90.8	90.7
15-17	87.1	90.7	90.6	90.7
Social class				
SC 1-2	91.1	93.7	94.0	93.9
SC 3-4	87.7	90.8	90.2	90.5
SC 5-6	86.0	88.8	88.2	88.5

Source: HBSC Survey, Health Promotion Research Centre

Differences by geographic location

- Children in the Border and West regions were more likely to report feeling safe where they live (94.2%), while children in the Dublin region were least likely to report this (83.0%) (*see Table 114*). These differences were statistically significant.

Table 114: Percentage of children who report feeling safe in area where they live, by NUTS Region (2006)	
	%
All children	**90.4**
NUTS Region	
Border	94.2
Dublin	83.0
Midlands	91.2
Mid-East	89.6
Mid-West	93.6
South-East	92.1
South-West	91.5
West	94.2

Source: HBSC Survey, Health Promotion Research Centre

International comparisons

- From the 2006 HBSC Survey, using the ages of 11, 13 and 15 only to draw international comparisons, 91.2% of children from Ireland reported feeling safe in the area where they live (*see Figure 26*). This was significantly higher than the HBSC average of 89.5%.
- Among the 8 countries and regions that used this HBSC item in 2006, the lowest percentage for this indicator was found among children from Poland (82.2%) and the highest among children from Belgium (Flemish) (93.0%). Overall, children from Ireland ranked 3rd.

Figure 26: Percentage of children who report feeling safe in the area where they live, by country (2006)

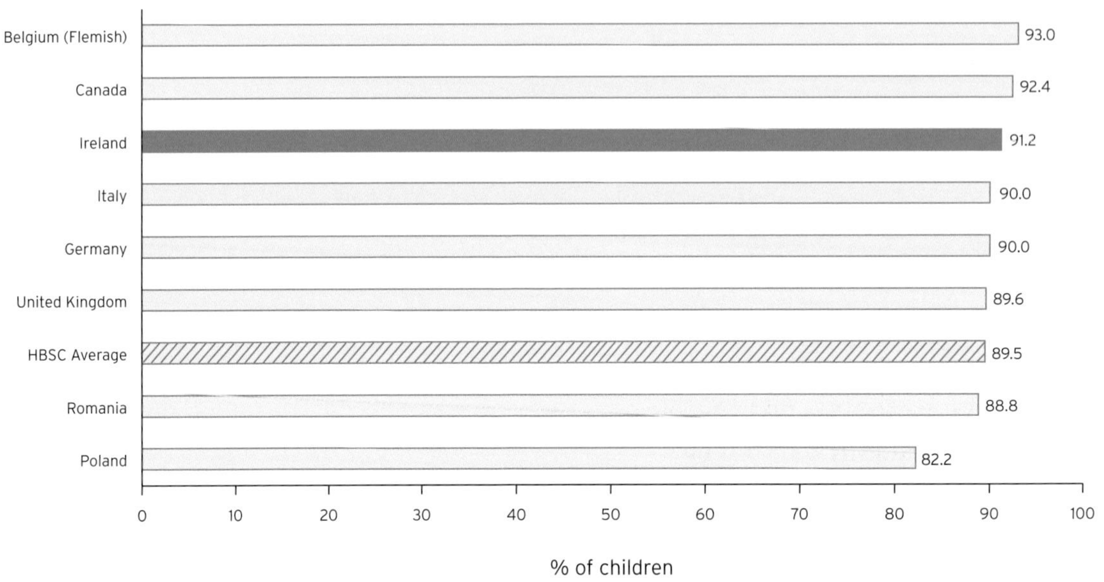

Source: HBSC Survey, Health Promotion Research Centre

ENVIRONMENT AND PLACES

Traveller children and immigrant children are more likely to report having good places in their area to spend their free time.

Measure

The percentage of children aged 9-17 who report there are good places in their area to spend their free time.

Key findings

- In 2006, 42.2% of children aged 9-17 reported that there were good places in their area to spend their free time.

Differences by population groups

- When compared to other children, Traveller children and immigrant children were more likely to report that there are good places in their area to spend their free time (*see Table 115*). These differences were statistically significant.
- There were no significant differences between children with and children without a disability and/or chronic illness.

Table 115: Percentage of children who report that there are good places in their area to spend their free time, by population groups (2006)	
	%
All children	**42.2**
Traveller status	
Traveller children	58.4
All other children	41.8
Immigrant status	
Immigrant children	48.7
All other children	41.9
Disability and/or Chronic Illness status	
Children with a disability and/or chronic illness	43.6
All other children	41.9

Source: HBSC Survey, Health Promotion Research Centre

Differences by age, gender, social class and over time

- Statistically significant differences were also observed across age, gender and social class categories, with a higher percentage of boys, younger children and children in the lowest social class category reporting that there are good places in their area where they can spend their free time (*see Table 116*).

Table 116: Percentage of children who report that there are good places in their area to spend their free time, by age, gender and social class (2002 and 2006)

	2002	2006		
	Total (%)	Boys (%)	Girls (%)	Total (%)
All children	**43.9**	**45.4**	**39.0**	**42.2**
Age				
9	–	75.9	78.3	77.1
10-11	59.6	56.6	54.9	55.6
12-14	47.5	49.7	41.9	45.9
15-17	32.6	37.6	28.5	33.3
Social class				
SC 1-2	43.0	42.0	35.0	38.6
SC 3-4	44.4	45.4	38.8	42.1
SC 5-6	44.1	49.1	41.7	45.2

Source: HBSC Survey, Health Promotion Research Centre

Differences by geographic location

- Children in the Dublin region were more likely to report that there are good places in their area where they can spend their free time (58.4%), while children in the West were least likely to report this (33.4%) (*see Table 117*). These differences were statistically significant.

Table 117: Percentage of children who report that there are good places in their area to spend their free time, by NUTS Region (2006)

	%
All children	**42.2**
NUTS Region	
Border	36.5
Dublin	58.4
Midlands	36.7
Mid-East	34.7
Mid-West	36.0
South-East	38.3
South-West	45.1
West	33.4

Source: HBSC Survey, Health Promotion Research Centre

International comparisons

- From the 2006 HBSC Survey, using the ages of 11, 13 and 15 only to draw international comparisons, 45.7% of children from Ireland reported that there are good places in their area to spend their free time (*see Figure 27*). This was significantly lower than the HBSC average of 64.3%
- Among the 7 countries and regions that used this HBSC item, the lowest percentage for this indicator was found among children from Ireland (45.7%) and the highest among children from Germany (75.7%).

Figure 27: Percentage of children who report that there are good places in their area to spend their free time, by country (2006)

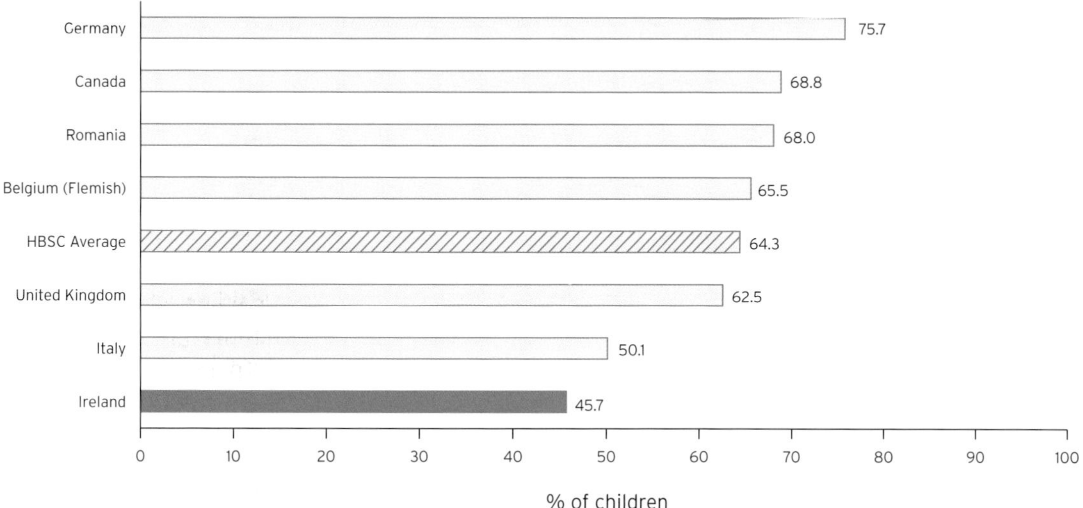

Source: HBSC Survey, Health Promotion Research Centre

GARDA JUVENILE DIVERSION PROGRAMME REFERRALS

There has been a substantial decrease in the number of children referred to the Garda Juvenile Diversion Programme.

Measure

The number of children aged 10-17 referred to the Garda Juvenile Diversion Programme.

Key findings

- In 2009, there were 18,519 children referred and 23,952 referrals to the Garda Juvenile Diversion Programme, a rate of 1.3 referrals per child referred.

Differences by age, gender, offence and over time

- 77.3% (18,525) of referrals were from children aged 15-17 years (*see Table 118*). This equates to a rate of 1,094.3 referrals per 10,000 children aged 15-17 years.
- 80.7% (14,950) of children referred to the Garda Juvenile Diversion Programme were boys and 19.3% (3,569) were girls.
- The majority of referrals were dealt with by way of a formal (22.3%) or informal (45.8%) caution, while 25.3% (6,050) were considered unsuitable. A referral is recorded as unsuitable if (a) the child does not accept responsibility for his or her behaviour, (b) the child is offending persistently or (c) it would not be in the interest of society to caution the child.
- Alcohol-related offences were the single highest cause of referrals to the Garda Juvenile Diversion Programme, representing 17.8% of all referrals (*see Figure 28*).
- Since 2008, there has been a substantial decrease in the number of children referred and in the number of referrals.

Table 118: Number, percentage and rate (per 10,000) of children aged 10-17 referred/referrals to the Garda Juvenile Diversion Programme, by age, gender and outcome (2005-2009)

	2005	2006	2007	2008	2009		
	No.	No.	No.	No.	No.	%	Rate per 10,000
Total number of children	**17,567**	**20,016**	**21,941**	**21,412**	**18,519**	**100.0**	**404.9**
Gender							
Boys	13,933	16,257	17,802	17,195	14,950	80.7	637.6
Girls	3,634	3,759	4,139	4,217	3,569	19.3	160.1
Total number of referrals	**21,497**	**25,080**	**27,853**	**27,422**	**23,952**	**100.0**	**523.7**
Age							
10-14	6,067	6,582	6,543	6,278	5,427	22.7	188.4
15-17	15,430	18,498	21,310	21,144	18,525	77.3	1,094.3
Outcome							
Formal	3,677	4,687	5,291	5,108	5,345	22.3	116.9
Informal	10,999	12,225	13,651	12,884	10,979	45.8	240.1
No further action	1,073	1,380	1,275	1,682	946	3.9	20.7
Pending	1,143	939	1,084	732	632	2.6	13.8
Not suitable	4,605	5,849	6,552	7,016	6,050	25.3	132.3

Source: An Garda Síochána

Figure 28: Percentage referrals to the Garda Juvenile Diversion Programme, by type of offence (2009)

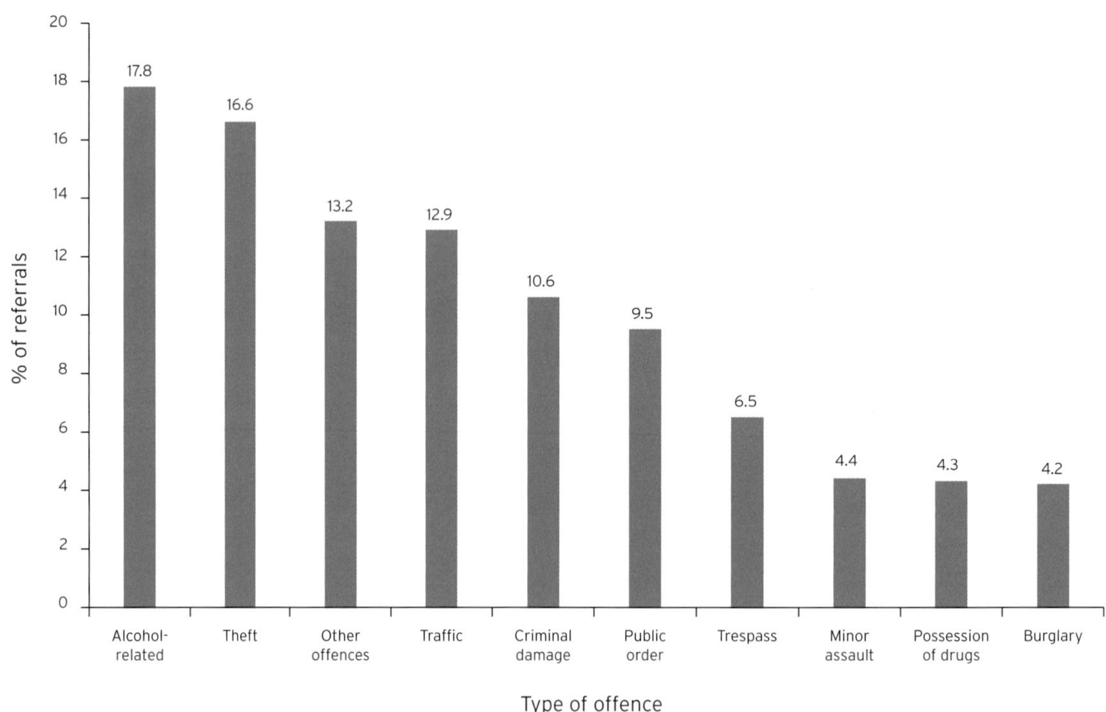

Source: An Garda Síochána

Differences by geographic location

- Almost one-third (32.4%) of all referrals and of all children referred to the Garda Juvenile Diversion Programme were in the Dublin Metropolitan Region (*see Table 119*).

Table 119: Number and percentage of children aged 10-17 referred/referrals to the Garda Juvenile Diversion Programme, by Region and Division (2009)

	Total number of children referred		Total number of referrals	
	No.	%	No.	%
Total	**18,519**	**100.0**	**23,952**	**100.0**
Eastern Region	**2,488**	**13.4**	**3,163**	**13.2**
Kildare	546	2.9	670	2.8
Laois/Offaly	574	3.1	744	3.1
Meath	472	2.5	618	2.6
Westmeath	339	1.8	450	1.9
Wicklow	557	3.0	681	2.8
Dublin Metropolitan Region (DMR)	**6,006**	**32.4**	**7,769**	**32.4**
DMR East	610	3.3	735	3.1
DMR North	1,633	8.8	2,086	8.7
DMR North Central	451	2.4	676	2.8
DMR South	1,309	7.1	1,708	7.1
DMR South Central	358	1.9	464	1.9
DMR West	1,645	8.9	2,100	8.8
Northern Region	**1,961**	**10.6**	**2,505**	**10.5**
Cavan/Monaghan	518	2.8	672	2.8
Donegal	626	3.4	778	3.2
Louth	537	2.9	720	3.0
Sligo/Leitrim	280	1.5	335	1.4
South-Eastern Region	**2,159**	**11.7**	**2,900**	**12.1**
Kilkenny/Carlow	486	2.6	641	2.7
Tipperary	557	3.0	737	3.1
Waterford	670	3.6	919	3.8
Wexford	446	2.4	603	2.5

continued

Table 119 *(continued)*

	Total number of children referred		Total number of referrals	
	No.	%	No.	%
Southern Region	**3,780**	**20.4**	**5,009**	**20.9**
Cork City	1,230	6.6	1,595	6.7
Cork North	657	3.5	844	3.5
Cork West	432	2.3	603	2.5
Kerry	510	2.8	653	2.7
Limerick	951	5.1	1,314	5.5
Western Region	**2,072**	**11.2**	**2,545**	**10.6**
Clare	379	2.0	462	1.9
Galway	844	4.6	1,021	4.3
Mayo	510	2.8	665	2.8
Roscommon/Longford	339	1.8	397	1.7
Outside jurisdiction	53	0.3	61	0.3

Source: An Garda Síochána

ANTENATAL CARE

Early antenatal care is lowest among younger mothers.

Measure

The percentage of mothers attending for antenatal care in the first trimester of pregnancy.

Key findings

- In 2008, 70.4% of women attended for antenatal care in the first trimester of pregnancy.

Differences by age, social class and over time

- Antenatal care in the first trimester of pregnancy is lowest among mothers aged 15-19 (56.3%) (*see Table 120*).
- Women who were primarily engaged in 'home duties' also had one of the lowest percentages of antenatal visits in the first trimester of pregnancy (62.5%) (*see Figure 29*).

Table 120: Percentage of mothers attending for antenatal care in the first trimester of pregnancy, by mothers' age (2004-2008)*

	2004	2005	2006	2007	2008
Total	**68.3**	**71.5**	**72.8**	**70.9**	**70.4**
Age					
15-19	56.8	61.2	62.3	57.4	56.3
20-24	61.8	65.8	65.2	62.4	61.9
25-29	66.8	71.0	72.9	69.4	68.3
30-34	71.7	74.4	75.6	74.1	73.6
35-39	71.2	73.2	74.6	74.1	74.4
40-44	68.3	70.0	72.5	73.8	72.3
45 and over	68.9	64.5	53.6	64.2	70.9

* Categories where percentages are based on less than 100 births (i.e. 'under 15 years' and 'age not stated') have been omitted from this Table.

Source: National Perinatal Reporting System, ESRI

Figure 29: Percentage of mothers attending for antenatal care in the first trimester of pregnancy, by mothers' occupation (2008)*

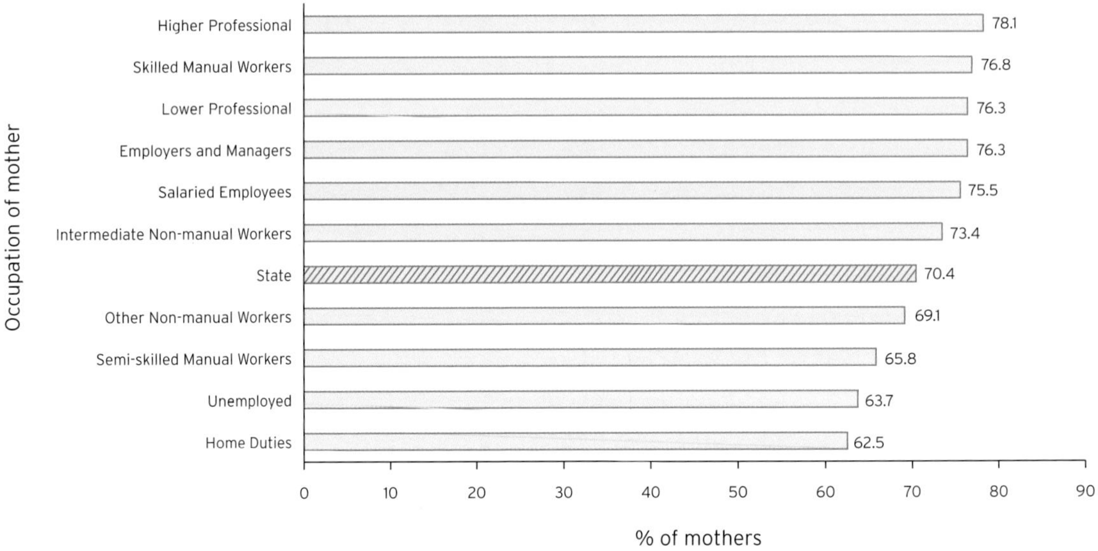

* Categories where percentages are based on less than 100 births (i.e. 'unskilled manual workers', 'other agricultural occupations and fishermen', 'farmers and farm managers') and 'not stated' and 'not classifiable' categories have been omitted from this Figure.

Source: National Perinatal Reporting System, ESRI

Differences by geographic location

- 91.7% of women in Donegal attended for antenatal care in the first trimester of pregnancy, compared to 33.2% of women in Louth *(see FIgure 30)*. This may be due, in part at least, to some differences in recording first contact with General Practitioner (GP) services.

Figure 30: Percentage of mothers attending for antenatal care in the first trimester of pregnancy, by mothers' county of residence (2008)*

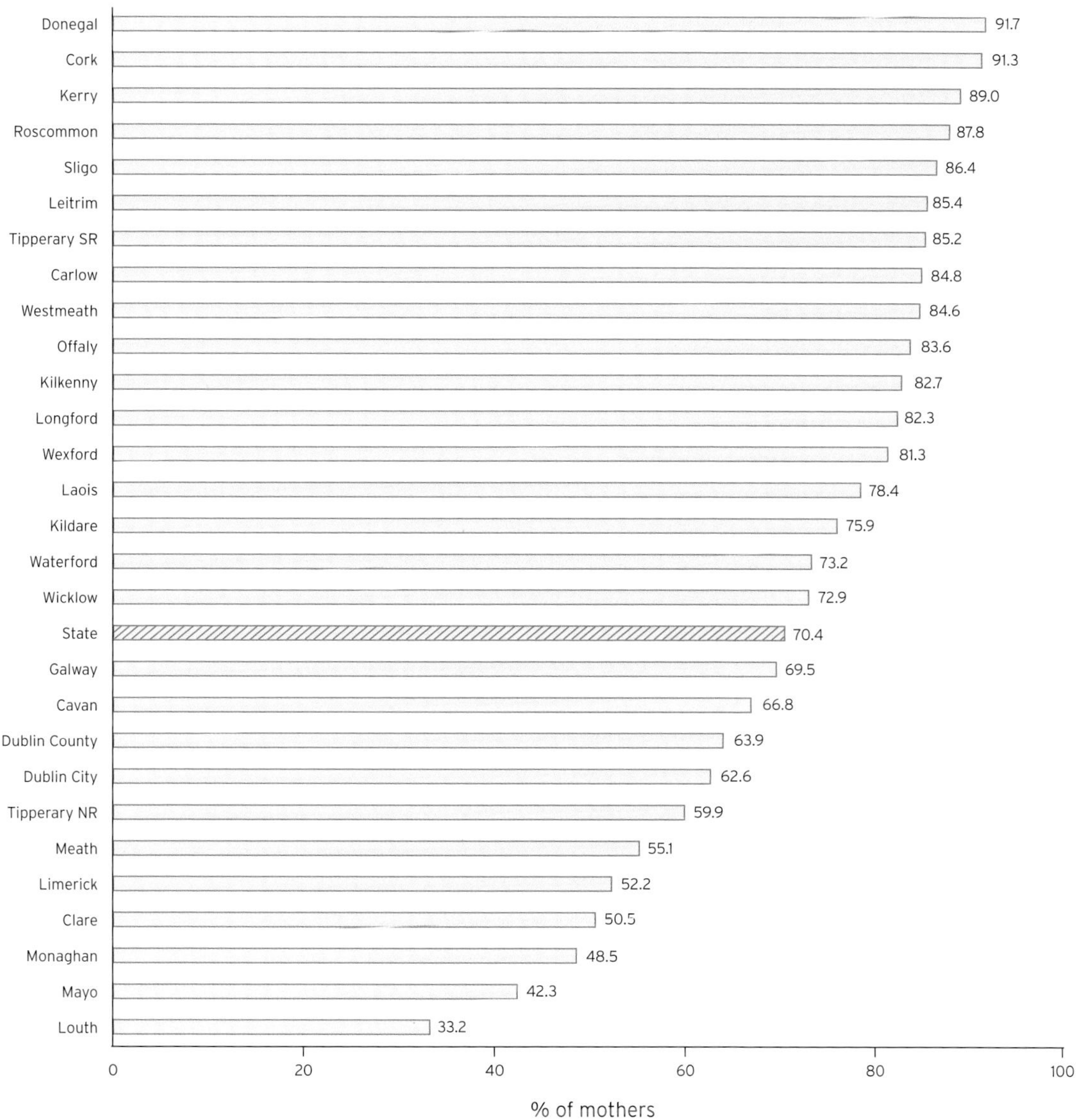

* Categories where percentages are based on less than 100 births (i.e. 'other' and 'not stated') have been omitted from this Figure.

Source: National Perinatal Reporting System, ESRI

CHILDHOOD IMMUNISATION

In 2009, Roscommon had the highest uptake of the recommended doses of all vaccines among children at 12 and 24 months.

Measure

The percentage uptake of the recommended doses of vaccines among children at (a) 12 months and (b) 24 months of age.

List of vaccines presented below (see technical notes in Appendix 1 for immunisation schedule):

D_3	3 doses of vaccine against diphtheria
P_3	3 doses of vaccine against pertussis
T_3	3 doses of vaccine against tetanus
Hib_3	3 doses of vaccine against *Haemophilus influenzae* type b
$Polio_3$	3 doses of vaccine against polio
$HepB_3$	3 doses of vaccine against hepatitis B
$MenC_3$	3 doses of vaccine against meningococcal group C
$MenC_2$	2 doses of vaccine against meningococcal group C
PCV_2	2 doses of vaccine against pneumococcal conjugate vaccine
Hib_b	1 booster dose of vaccine against *Haemophilus influenzae* type b
MMR_1	1 dose of vaccine against measles, mumps and rubella
BCG	1 dose of Bacillus Calmette-Guerin vaccine

Key findings

- In 2009, the national uptake rates (based on available data) for children at **12 months** of age were 89% for D_3, P_3, T_3, Hib_3 and $Polio_3$; 95% for BCG; 86% for $MenC_3$ (based on Quarters 1 and 2 2009 data only); and 89% for $HepB_3$, $MenC_2$ and PCV_2 (based on available data in Quarters 3 and 4 2009 only).
- The national uptake rates (based on available data) for children at **24 months** of age were 94% for D_3, P_3, T_3 and $Polio_3$; 93% for $MenC_3$ and Hib_3; 90% for MMR_1; and 87% for Hib_b.

Differences by age, vaccine type and over time

- Over the period 2005-2009, for children at **12 months** of age the national uptake rates (based on available data) have increased, from 85% to 89% for D_3, P_3, T_3, Hib_3 and $Polio_3$; and from 93% to 95% for BCG (*see Table 121*).
- Over the same period, for children at **24 months** of age the national uptake rates (based on available data) have increased, from 89% to 93% for $MenC_3$; from 90% to 94% for D_3, P_3, T_3 and $Polio_3$; from 90% to 93% for Hib_3; and from 84% to 90% for MMR_1.

Table 121: Immunisation uptake rates, by age and vaccine type (2005-2009)*

	2005	2006	2007	2008	2009
At 12 months					
BCG	93	93	93	94	95
D_3	85	86	87	88	89
P_3	85	86	87	88	89
T_3	85	86	87	88	89
Hib_3	85	86	87	88	89
$Polio_3$	85	86	87	88	89
$MenC_3$	85	85	87	88	86
$HepB_3$	*n/a*	*n/a*	*n/a*	*n/a*	89
$MenC_2$	*n/a*	*n/a*	*n/a*	*n/a*	89
PCV_2	*n/a*	*n/a*	*n/a*	*n/a*	89
At 24 months					
D_3	90	91	92	93	94
P_3	90	91	92	93	94
T_3	90	91	92	93	94
Hib_3	90	91	92	93	93
Hib_b	*n/a*	*n/a*	74	82	87
$Polio_3$	90	91	92	93	94
$MenC_3$	89	90	91	92	93
MMR_1	84	86	87	89	90

n/a = not applicable (*see below*)

* Please see technical notes in Appendix 1 for caveats to data (as a number of figures presented here are incomplete) and for changes to the primary childhood immunisation schedule introduced on 1st September 2008.

Source: Immunisation Uptake Statistics, Health Protection Surveillance Centre

Differences by geographic location

- For children at **12 months** of age, uptake rates among Local Health Offices (LHOs) (based on available data) for D_3, T_3, P_3 and $Polio_3$ ranged from 82% to 96%; Hib_3 ranged from 82% to 95%; and $MenC_3$ ranged from 76% to 94% (based on Quarters 1 and 2 2009 data only) (*see Table 122*). Based on available data in Quarters 3 and 4 2009 only, $HepB_3$ ranged from 84% to 95%; $MenC_2$ ranged from 82% to 95%; and PCV_2 ranged from 82% to 96%. The target uptake of 95% was reached or exceeded in Roscommon for D_3, P_3, T_3, Hib_3, $Polio_3$, $HepB_3$, $MenC_2$ and PCV_2.

Table 122: Immunisation uptake rates at 12 months, by HSE Region and Local Health Office (LHO) Area (2009)*

	Immunisation uptake (%)							
	BCG	$D_3P_3T_3$	Hib_3	$Polio_3$	$MenC_3$	$HepB_3$	$MenC_2$	PCV_2
Total	**95**	**89**	**89**	**89**	**86**	**89**	**89**	**89**
HSE Dublin North East	***n/a***	**89**	**89**	**89**	**86**	**90**	**89**	**88**
Cavan/Monaghan	*n/a*	93	93	93	88	94	93	91
Dublin North	*n/a*	89	89	89	87	89	88	89
Dublin North Central	*n/a*	90	89	90	85	90	88	88
Dublin North West	*n/a*	84	84	84	81	84	82	82
Louth	*n/a*	91	91	91	87	91	89	88
Meath	*n/a*	91	91	91	87	92	91	89
HSE Dublin Mid-Leinster	**94**	**88**	**87**	**88**	**85**	**88**	**88**	**88**
Dublin South	*n/a*	91	91	91	90	88	90	89
Dublin South City	*n/a*	85	85	85	76	90	89	89
Dublin South East	*n/a*	93	93	93	89	92	91	90
Dublin South West	*n/a*	93	92	93	90	92	91	92
Dublin West	*n/a*	85	85	85	82	86	86	85
Kildare/West Wicklow	*n/a*	82	82	82	77	86	86	86
Laois/Offaly	95	92	92	92	92	*n/a*	*n/a*	*n/a*
Longford/Westmeath	94	94	94	94	94	*n/a*	*n/a*	*n/a*
Wicklow	*n/a*	87	87	87	85	87	87	87

continued

Table 122 *(continued)*

	Immunisation uptake (%)							
	BCG	$D_3P_3T_3$	Hib_3	$Polio_3$	$MenC_3$	$HepB_3$	$MenC_2$	PCV_2
HSE South	**95**	**88**	**88**	**88**	**87**	**90**	**90**	**90**
Carlow/Kilkenny	95	88	88	88	87	88	87	87
Kerry	93	83	83	83	82	*n/a*	*n/a*	*n/a*
North Cork	*n/a*	87	87	87	87	*n/a*	*n/a*	*n/a*
North Lee/South Lee**	*n/a*	87	87	87	87	*n/a*	*n/a*	*n/a*
Tipperary SR	95	91	91	91	91	92	91	91
Waterford	95	89	89	89	87	89	89	89
West Cork	*n/a*	82	82	82	82	*n/a*	*n/a*	*n/a*
Wexford	96	91	91	91	89	92	92	92
HSE West	**96**	**90**	**90**	**90**	**89**	**89**	**88**	**90**
Clare	98	91	91	91	89	93	*n/a*	93
Donegal	94	92	92	92	91	91	91	92
Galway	*n/a*	87	87	87	85	86	87	87
Limerick	97	90	90	90	87	92	*n/a*	91
Mayo	*n/a*	88	88	88	87	88	86	88
Roscommon	*n/a*	96	95	96	94	95	95	96
Sligo/Leitrim/West Cavan	96	91	91	91	91	88	87	88
Tipperary NR	96	91	91	91	91	91	*n/a*	92

n/a = not applicable (*see below*)

* Please see technical notes in Appendix 1 for caveats to data (as a number of figures presented here are incomplete) and for changes to the primary childhood immunisation schedule introduced on 1st September 2008.

** While North Lee and South Lee are two separate LHOs, their combined immunisation uptake data are reported here.

Source: Immunisation Uptake Statistics, Health Protection Surveillance Centre

- For children at **24 months** of age, uptake rates among Local Health Offices (LHOs) (based on available data) for D_3, T_3, P_3, Hib_3, $Polio_3$ and $MenC_3$ ranged from 89% to 98%; Hib_b ranged from 78% to 98%; and MMR_1 ranged from 84% to 97% (*see Table 123*). Again, Roscommon had the highest uptake of the recommended doses of all vaccines.

Table 123: Immunisation uptake rates at 24 months, by HSE Region and Local Health Office (LHO) Area (2009)*						
	Immunisation uptake (%)					
	$D_3P_3T_3$	Hib_3	Hib_b	$Polio_3$	$MenC_3$	MMR_1
Total	**94**	**93**	**87**	**94**	**93**	**90**
HSE Dublin North East	**94**	**93**	**88**	**94**	**94**	**90**
Cavan/Monaghan	95	95	92	95	96	92
Dublin North Central	95	94	83	95	93	90
Dublin North West	92	91	85	92	92	87
Dublin North	94	93	86	94	93	91
Louth	93	93	92	93	95	91
Meath	94	94	92	94	95	92
HSE Dublin Mid-Leinster	**93**	**93**	**85**	**93**	**93**	**89**
Dublin South	97	96	87	97	96	93
Dublin South City	90	89	78	90	89	84
Dublin South East	97	97	86	97	97	93
Dublin South West	95	94	86	95	93	94
Dublin West	92	92	82	92	91	88
Kildare/West Wicklow	89	89	80	89	89	85
Laois/Offaly	95	95	92	95	95	92
Longford/Westmeath	97	97	94	97	97	94
Wicklow	92	91	81	92	91	85
HSE South	**93**	**93**	**89**	**93**	**93**	**90**
Carlow/Kilkenny	92	91	91	92	91	91
Kerry	92	92	84	92	91	87
North Cork	96	96	89	96	95	92
North Lee/South Lee**	95	95	90	95	95	92
Tipperary SR	93	93	90	93	92	90
Waterford	90	90	87	90	89	86
West Cork	90	90	82	90	89	84
Wexford	94	94	92	94	93	91

continued

Table 123 *(continued)*

	Immunisation uptake (%)					
	$D_3P_3T_3$	Hib_3	Hib_b	$Polio_3$	$MenC_3$	MMR_1
HSE West	**94**	**94**	**89**	**94**	**94**	**91**
Clare	93	93	89	93	93	92
Donegal	96	96	93	96	95	92
Galway	94	94	86	94	93	90
Limerick	92	92	86	92	92	89
Mayo	93	93	82	93	93	87
Roscommon	98	98	98	98	98	97
Sligo/Leitrim/West Cavan	96	96	93	97	94	93
Tipperary NR	96	95	91	96	95	94

* Please see technical notes in Appendix 1 for caveats to data (as a number of figures presented here are incomplete) and for changes to the primary childhood immunisation schedule introduced on 1st September 2008.

** While North Lee and South Lee are two separate LHOs, their combined immunisation uptake data are reported here.

Source: Immunisation Uptake Statistics, Health Protection Surveillance Centre

International comparisons

- Uptake rates of the recommended doses of vaccines among children of relevant age for D_3, P_3, T_3 and $Polio_3$ reported in countries across the EU-27 ranged from 73% in Malta to 100% in Hungary (*see Table 124*). Hungary also reported a 100% uptake rate of a measles-containing vaccine.

Table 124: Immunisation uptake rates among children of relevant age, by vaccine type and EU-27 (2009)			
	$D_3P_3T_3$	$Polio_3$	Measles-containing vaccine
Country			
Austria	83	83	76
Belgium	99	99	94
Bulgaria	94	94	96
Cyprus	99	99	87
Czech Republic	99	99	*n/a*
Denmark	89	89	84
Estonia	95	95	95
Finland	99	99	99
France	99	*n/a*	90
Germany	*n/a*	96	96
Greece	99	99	99
Hungary	100	100	100
Ireland	**94**	**94**	**90**
Italy	*n/a*	*n/a*	*n/a*
Latvia	95	96	96
Lithuania	98	98	96
Luxembourg	99	99	96
Malta	73	73	82
Netherlands	97	*n/a*	96
Norway	93	93	92
Poland	99	96	98
Portugal	96	96	95
Romania	*n/a*	*n/a*	*n/a*
Slovakia	99	99	99
Slovenia	96	96	95
Spain	96	96	98
Sweden	98	98	97
United Kingdom	93	93	86

n/a = *not available*

Source: Centralised Information System for Infectious Diseases, WHO

ACCESSIBILITY OF BASIC HEALTH SERVICES

In April 2010, 2,591 children were known to be on a hospital waiting list.

Measure

The number of children on hospital waiting lists.

Key findings

- In April 2010, 2,591 children were known to be on a hospital waiting list awaiting treatment.

Differences by waiting time and speciality

- 47.8% (1,238) of these children were on the hospital list for 3-6 months, 43.5% (1,128) for 6-12 months and 8.7% (225) for 1 year or more (*see Table 125*).
- Of the 2,591 children who were known to be on a hospital waiting list awaiting treatment, 88.8% (2,302) were awaiting surgical treatment and 11.2% (289) were awaiting medical treatment.

Differences by geographic location

- Hospitals in Dublin accounted for approximately 60% of the total number of children waiting for treatment (1,563) (*see Table 125*).

Table 125: Number of children on hospital waiting lists (surgical and medical), by hospital and waiting time (2010)				
	3-6 months	6-12 months	Over 12 months	Total
Total	**1,238**	**1,128**	**225**	**2,591**
Hospital				
Beaumont Hospital, Dublin	9	2	1	12
Cappagh Orthopaedic Hospital	2	1	0	3
Cavan General Hospital	2	0	0	2
Children's University Hospital Temple Street, Dublin	181	176	79	436
Cork University Hospital	30	42	4	76
Kerry General Hospital	3	0	0	3
Letterkenny General Hospital	7	2	0	9
Mercy University Hospital, Cork	19	29	0	48
Merlin Park Hospital, Galway	1	1	0	2
Midland Regional Hospital, Mullingar	0	1	0	1
Midland Regional Hospital, Portlaoise	2	0	0	2
Midland Regional Hospital, Tullamore	102	37	2	141
Mid-Western Regional Hospital, Dooradoyle	36	17	8	61
Monaghan General Hospital	37	38	0	75
Our Lady of Lourdes Hospital, Drogheda	129	46	10	185
Our Lady's Hospital for Sick Children, Crumlin	401	505	116	1,022
Royal Victoria Eye and Ear Hospital, Dublin	6	3	0	9
Sligo General Hospital	38	29	2	69
South Infirmary Victoria University Hospital, Cork	6	2	0	8
St. John's Hospital, Limerick	1	0	2	3
St. Luke's General Hospital, Kilkenny	2	0	0	2
Tallaght Hospital (AMNCH), Dublin	60	20	1	81
University College Hospital, Galway	115	149	0	264
Waterford Regional Hospital	49	28	0	77

Source: Patient Treatment Register, National Treatment Purchase Fund

CHILDREN AND YOUNG PEOPLE IN CARE

Almost 9 out of 10 children in the care of the Health Service Executive live in foster family homes.

Measure

The number of children who are in the care of the Health Service Executive (HSE).

Key findings

- In 2008, 5,357 children were in the care of the HSE.

Differences by age, gender, type placement, length of stay and over time

- 50.7% (2,717) of children in the care of the HSE were boys and 49.3% (2,640) were girls (*see Table 126*).
- The majority of children (88.5%) in the care of the HSE lived with foster families and more than one in 3 (36.2%) were in care for a period of 5 years or more.
- Over the period 2006-2008, the number of children in the care of the HSE has increased.

Table 126: Number and percentage of children in the care of the HSE, by age, gender, type of placement and length of stay (2006-2008)				
	2006	2007	2008	
	No.	No.	No.	%
Total	**5,247**	**5,307**	**5,357**	**100.0**
Age				
0-4	852	819	834	15.6
5-9	1,420	1,434	1,452	27.1
10-14	1,764	1,780	1,799	33.6
15-17	1,211	1,274	1,272	23.7
Gender				
Boys	2,681	2,695	2,717	50.7
Girls	2,566	2,612	2,640	49.3
Type of placement				
Foster Care – General	3,073	3,141	3,134	58.5
Foster Care – Special	40	31	27	0.5
Foster Care – Relative	1,482	1,552	1,581	29.5
Pre-adoptive placement	36	26	24	0.4
Residential – General	351	337	328	6.1
Residential – Special Care	16	21	30	0.6
Residential – High Support	41	30	23	0.4
At home under Care Order	44	41	38	0.7
Other	164	128	172	3.2
Length of stay				
Less than 1 year	1,414	1,339	1,236	23.1
1-5 years	2,069	1,985	2,181	40.7
5 years or more	1,764	1,983	1,940	36.2

Source: Child Care Interim Data Set, HSE

Differences by geographic location

- The highest number and percentage of children in the care of the HSE was in the Dublin North West Local Health Office (LHO) Area in the HSE Dublin North East Region (*see Table 127*). This was followed by the North Lee LHO Area in the HSE South Region.

Table 127: Number and percentage of children in the care of the HSE, by HSE Region and Local Health Office (LHO) Area (2008)

	No.	%
Total	**5,357**	**100.0**
HSE Dublin North East	**1,396**	**26.1**
Cavan/Monaghan	152	2.8
Dublin North	137	2.6
Dublin North Central	356	6.6
Dublin North West	430	8.0
Louth	178	3.3
Meath	143	2.7
HSE Dublin Mid-Leinster	**1,456**	**27.2**
Dublin South	141	2.6
Dublin South City	141	2.6
Dublin South East	102	1.9
Dublin South West	183	3.4
Dublin West	214	4.0
Kildare/West Wicklow	209	3.9
Laois/Offaly	202	3.8
Longford/Westmeath	116	2.2
Wicklow	148	2.8

continued

Table 127 *(continued)*		
	No.	**%**
HSE South	**1,471**	**27.5**
Carlow/Kilkenny	148	2.8
Kerry	130	2.4
North Cork	78	1.5
North Lee	363	6.8
South Lee	190	3.5
Tipperary SR	134	2.5
Waterford	187	3.5
West Cork	61	1.1
Wexford	180	3.4
HSE West	**1,034**	**19.3**
Clare	126	2.4
Donegal	124	2.3
Galway	170	3.2
Limerick	225	4.2
Mayo	111	2.1
Roscommon	121	2.3
Sligo/Leitrim/West Cavan	76	1.4
Tipperary NR	81	1.5

Source: Child Care Interim Data Set, HSE

MENTAL HEALTH REFERRALS

There has been an increase in the number of children admitted to psychiatric hospitals.

Measure

The number of admissions to psychiatric hospitals among children.

Key findings

- In 2008, there were 406 admissions to psychiatric hospitals among children. This equates to an overall rate of 37.4 children per 100,000.

Differences by age, gender, diagnosis and over time

- 84.0% (341) of children admitted to psychiatric hospitals were aged 15-17 years (*see Table 128*).
- 41.9% (170) of children admitted to psychiatric hospitals were boys and 58.1% (236) were girls. This equates to a rate of 30.6 per 100,000 boys and 44.6 per 100,000 girls.
- The most common reason for children being admitted to psychiatric hospitals was for 'neuroses' (33.7%), followed by 'depressive disorders' (26.1%) Other common reasons included 'personality disorders' (7.4%) and 'other psychoses' (6.9%).
- Over the period 2004-2008, the number of admissions to psychiatric hospitals among children ranged from 333 in 2005 to 406 in 2008.

Table 128: Number, percentage and rate (per 100,000) of admissions to psychiatric hospitals among children, by age, gender and diagnosis (2004-2008)

	2004	2005	2006	2007	2008		
	No.	No.	No.	No.	No.	%	Rate per 100,000
Total	**352**	**333**	**398**	**364**	**406**	**100.0**	**37.4**
Age							
0-4	0	0	0	0	0	0.0	0.0
5-9	5	1	4	4	3	0.7	1.0
10-14	38	46	61	72	62	15.3	22.1
15-17	309	286	333	288	341	84.0	197.0
Gender							
Boys	185	181	218	153	170	41.9	30.6
Girls	167	152	180	211	236	58.1	44.6
Diagnosis							
Alcoholic disorders	17	13	17	12	8	2.0	0.7
Depressive disorders	79	88	118	90	106	26.1	9.8
Drug dependence	32	33	23	15	17	4.2	1.6
Mania	22	11	23	18	21	5.2	1.9
Mental handicap	5	6	1	2	2	0.5	0.2
Neuroses	75	63	56	104	137	33.7	12.6
Organic psychoses	7	5	15	12	3	0.7	0.3
Other psychoses	13	14	19	10	28	6.9	2.6
Personality disorders	40	36	29	21	30	7.4	2.8
Schizophrenia	27	30	32	27	13	3.2	1.2
Unspecified	35	34	65	53	41	10.1	3.8

Source: National Psychiatric In-Patient Reporting System (NPIRS), Health Research Board

Differences by geographic location

- 23.2% of children admitted to psychiatric hospitals were from Dublin (*see Table 129*).

Table 129: Number and percentage of admissions to psychiatric hospitals among children, by county (2008)

	No.	%
Total	**406**	**100.0**
County		
Carlow	7	1.7
Cavan	6	1.5
Clare	5	1.2
Cork City and County	25	6.2
Donegal	9	2.2
Dublin	94	23.2
Galway City and County	24	5.9
Kerry	19	4.7
Kildare	20	4.9
Kilkenny	5	1.2
Laois	10	2.5
Leitrim	4	1.0
Limerick City and County	24	5.9
Longford	3	0.7
Louth	2	0.5
Mayo	14	3.4
Meath	20	4.9
Monaghan	3	0.7
Offaly	8	2.0
Roscommon	2	0.5
Sligo	5	1.2
Tipperary	23	5.7
Waterford City and County	9	2.2
Westmeath	13	3.2
Wexford	32	7.9
Wicklow	19	4.7
England and Northern Ireland	1	0.3

Source: National Psychiatric In-Patient Reporting System (NPIRS), Health Research Board

APPENDIX 1: MAIN DATA SOURCES, DEFINITIONS AND RELEVANT TECHNICAL NOTES

Report of the Committee Appointed to Monitor the Effectiveness of the Diversion Programme: An Garda Síochána

The Report of the Committee Appointed to Monitor the Effectiveness of the Diversion Programme is published on an annual basis. The following indicator draws on data from this source:

- Number of children aged 10-17 referred/referrals to Garda Juvenile Diversion Programme.

Census of the Population and Population Estimates: Central Statistics Office

The Census of Population is conducted by the Central Statistics Office (CSO) on a quinquennial basis. The following indicators, which draw on data from this source, define children as 'all population under 18 years of age' when the data were collected. Figures are based on either place of usual residence and present on Census night or de facto presence on Census night:

- Number of children (de facto).
- Number of children living in a lone-parent household (usual residence and present).
- Percentage of children whose mothers have attained (a) primary, (b) lower secondary, (c) upper secondary or (d) third-level education (usual residence and present).
- Number of Traveller children (de facto).
- Number of foreign national children (usual residence and present).
- Number of children with a disability (de facto).

Parental education level data refer to the highest educational attainment of the mother rather than the head of household. Where no mother is present, the highest educational attainment of the father is used instead. The figures are based on responses to Question 23 of the 2006 Census, which distinguishes between the following main categories:

1. No formal education or just primary education.
2. Lower secondary education: Junior, Intermediate/Group Certificate, 'O' levels/GCSEs, NCVA Foundation Certificate, Basic Skills Training Certificate or equivalent.
3. Upper secondary: Leaving Certificate, 'A' levels, NCVA Level 1 Certificate or equivalent, Technical or Vocational qualification, both Upper Secondary and Technical or Vocational qualification.

4. Third level: Non-degree, primary degree, professional qualification (of Degree status at least), both a Degree and a Professional qualification, post-graduate Certificate or Diploma, post-graduate Degree (Masters) or Doctorate (PhD).

A person is classified as a **Traveller** in the 2006 Census if the answer is 'Irish Traveller' to Question 14: *'What is your ethnic or cultural background?'.*

A person is identified as a **foreign national** in the 2006 Census if the answer is not 'Irish' to Question 6: *'What is your nationality?'.*

A person is defined as having a **disability** if they answer 'Yes' to any of the 5 options in Question 15 or Question 16.

- Question 15: '*Do you have any of the following long-lasting conditions?*'
  - (a) Blindness, deafness or a severe vision or hearing impairment.
  - (b) A condition that substantially limits one or more basic physical activities, such as walking, climbing stairs, reaching, lifting or carrying.
  - (c) A learning or intellectual disability.
  - (d) A psychological or emotional condition.
  - (e) Other, including any chronic illness.

- Question 16: '*If Yes to any of the conditions specified in Question 15, do you have any difficulty in doing any of the following activities?*'
  - (a) Learning, remembering or concentrating.
  - (b) Dressing, bathing or getting around inside the home.
  - (c) Going outside the home alone to shop or visit a doctor's surgery.
  - (d) Working at a job or business or attending school or college.
  - (e) Participating in other activities, for example, leisure or using transport.

Childcare Interim Dataset: Health Service Executive

The Childcare Interim Dataset is an administrative data source managed by the Health Service Executive (HSE). The following indicators draw on data from this source:

- The number of separated children seeking asylum.
- The number of child welfare and protection reports that went to initial assessment.
- The number of confirmed child abuse cases.
- The number of children in the care of the HSE.

The number of **child welfare and protection reports that went to initial assessment** and **confirmed child abuse cases** are important measures of the incidence of child abuse and neglect in Ireland. It should be noted, however, that these are affected by a number of factors other than the actual incidence of abuse and neglect, and some caution is thus required in drawing conclusions concerning the overall prevalence of abuse and neglect for the following reasons: (1) some cases of abuse and neglect are never reported; (2) some incidents are reported more than once and several reports may relate to a single family; and (3) reports tend to increase for reasons unrelated to the actual prevalence of abuse and neglect, such as a highly publicised case or public awareness campaign.

Some caution should be adopted when comparing across HSE Regions because of differences in the way in which cases are recorded. Work is currently taking place on the development of consistent approaches across the HSE Regions.

Childcare Module: Quarterly National Household Survey: Central Statistics Office

The Childcare Module attached to Quarter 4 of 2007 of the Quarterly National Household Survey is conducted by the Central Statistics Office (CSO). This Module is administered to all households in which there were primary school-going children or pre-school children. The following indicators draw on data from this source:

- Percentage of children under 13 years of age who avail of non-parental childcare.
- Percentage of households with children under 13 years of age who report that they 'have access to high-quality, affordable childcare in the community'.

Households were asked to indicate from the following categories the main type of childcare for their pre-school and primary school-going children:

1. Child minded at home by me/my partner.
2. Unpaid relative or family friend.
3. Paid relative or family friend.
4. Paid childminder/au pair/nanny.
5. Work-based crèche.
6. Crèche/Montessori/playgroup/after-school facility.
7. Special needs facility.
8. Other.

'Childcare' was defined as types of childcare arrangements usually made by parents/guardians on a regular weekly basis during the working day (e.g. Monday to Friday, 7am-7pm, or similar, as applicable to the household).

'Pre-school' refers to children aged up to 5 years who are not attending primary school and a small number who have not stated if they are attending primary school.

'Primary school' refers to children aged between 4 and 12 years who are attending primary school and a small number aged 6 to 12 years who have not stated if they are attending primary school or who have stated that they are not attending primary school.

Department of Education and Skills

The following indicators draw on data from the Department of Education and Skills:

- Percentage of children leaving national school by destination.
- Public expenditure on education.

Children leaving national school by destination are drawn from the school-based returns collated by the Department of Education and Skills. Tables refer to children leaving ordinary classes in national schools.

Non-capital **public expenditure on education** includes direct public expenditure on educational institutions, public subsidies to other private entities for education matters and public subsidies to households, such as scholarships and loans to students for tuition fees and student living costs.

The expenditure has been deflated to real prices by using the National Accounts series for net expenditure by Central and Local Government on current goods and services at base year 2008.

Public expenditure on education as used for the international comparison includes both current and capital expenditure.

In the mid-1990s, undergraduate tuition fees were abolished in Ireland.

Educational institutions are defined as entities that provide instructional services to individuals or education-related services to individuals and other educational institutions.

International data are collected through the joint UNESCO-OECD-Eurostat data collection questionnaires on educational finance. Countries provide data, coming usually from administrative sources on the basis of commonly agreed definitions.

Data on total public expenditure on education are expressed as a percentage of Gross Domestic Product (GDP). GDP is the central aggregate of National Accounts. It represents the total value added (output) in the production of goods and services in the country.

National public expenditure as a percentage of GDP is calculated using figures in national currency both for public expenditure and for GDP. European averages are weighted and therefore take into account the relative proportion of the student population or the education expenditure of the considered countries. They are calculated taking into account all relevant countries for which data are available. They are considered of sufficient quality if countries with available data exceed 70% of the population or of the GDP of the European aggregate.

GDP less net primary incomes from abroad less EU taxes plus EU subsidies is equal to Gross National Income (GNI). As can be seen from Table A1-1, Ireland is almost unique among EU countries in the level of divergence between GDP and GNI. Therefore in tables comparing expenditure across EU countries, Irish expenditure is shown under two measures - % of GDP and % of GNI - to reflect this situation.

Table A1-1: EU - Gross Domestic Product (GDP) and Gross National Income (GNI) at current market prices, by country (2009)

Country	GDP €bn	GNI €bn	GNI as % of GDP
Luxembourg	37.8	25.9	68.7
Ireland	**159.6**	**132.6**	**83.1**
Malta	5.7	5.3	93.4
Czech Republic	137.2	129.1	94.1
Hungary	93.1	87.6	94.1
Portugal	167.6	162.0	96.6
Poland	310.1	300.0	96.7
Greece	237.5	230.9	97.2
Estonia	13.7	13.4	97.7
Netherlands	570.2	557.1	97.7
Bulgaria	33.9	33.1	97.7
Spain	1,051.2	1,031.4	98.1
Romania	115.9	113.7	98.2
Cyprus	16.9	16.6	98.2
Italy	1,520.9	1,494.6	98.3
Slovenia	34.9	34.4	98.5

continued

Table A1-1 *(continued)*

Country	GDP €bn	GNI €bn	GNI as % of GDP
Slovakia	63.3	62.6	98.8
Austria	277.1	274.2	99.0
Lithuania	26.6	26.5	99.3
EU-27	**11,802.5**	**11,749.7**	**99.6**
Finland	171.0	170.9	99.9
Belgium	337.3	340.0	100.8
France	1,907.1	1,922.8	100.8
Germany	2,409.1	2,444.0	101.4
Sweden	292.7	298.0	101.8
United Kingdom	1,566.7	1,598.1	102.0
Denmark	222.9	229.4	102.9
Latvia	18.5	20.0	107.8

ECCE Database: Office of the Minister for Children and Youth Affairs

The Early Childhood Care and Education (ECCE) Database is an administrative data source managed by the Office of the Minister for Children and Youth Affairs. This was established in 2010 to monitor the Free Pre-School Year (ECCE) Scheme. The following indicator draws on data from this source:

- Percentage of Early Childhood Care and Education (ECCE) services under contract to deliver the Free Pre-School Year Scheme that meet basic and higher capitation criteria.

The Free Pre-School Year (ECCE) Scheme provides every child in the eligible age cohort (i.e. participating children must normally be more than 3 years 2 months and less than 4 years 7 months in September of the relevant year) with up to 15 hours per week of free early childhood care and education provision for 38 weeks per year. Pre-school services are contracted by the State to provide the free pre-school year on the basis of meeting a number of criteria, including qualification of staff. Two capitation rates are available:

- The **basic capitation rate** requires the following qualification profile:

  Pre-School Leaders must hold certification for a major award in childcare/early education at a minimum of Level 5 on the National Framework of Qualifications of Ireland (NFQ) or an equivalent nationally recognised qualification or a higher award in the childcare/early education field.

In recognition of the unprecedented nature of these criteria, an interim measure was provided for whereby services could be contracted to deliver the Free Pre-school Year Scheme if they could meet the following criteria:

> During the period September 2010 to August 2012, the qualification requirement will be considered to be met where a person can demonstrate that he or she has achieved a certification for an award in ECCE that includes significant content covering the core knowledge areas, child development, early learning, health and welfare, and has at least 2 years' experience of working in a position of responsibility with children in the 0-6 age range.

- The **higher capitation rate** is awarded based on the following criteria:

> A higher capitation fee, equivalent to €75 per week for 38 weeks, will be payable to playschool sessional service providers where all Pre-school Leaders hold a Bachelor degree in childcare/early education (minimum of Level 7 on the National Framework of Qualifications (NFQ) or equivalent) and have 3 years' experience working in the sector, and where all Pre-school Assistants hold a relevant major award in childcare/early education at Level 5 on the NFQ or its equivalent.

The Free Pre-School Year (ECCE) Scheme commenced in January 2010, therefore data above for 2009/2010 pertains to the period January - June 2010. A full year will normally comprise data from September to June of the following year.

Data are collected by each City and County Childcare Committee. In some cases, larger counties will have both a City and County Committee, e.g. Cork. Dublin has a childcare committee for each Local Authority area, e.g. Fingal, Dun Laoghaire/Rathdown.

European Union Survey on Income and Living Conditions (EU-SILC): Central Statistics Office

The European Union Survey on Income and Living Conditions (EU-SILC) is conducted in Ireland by the Central Statistics Office. The EU-SILC collects information on poverty, deprivation and social exclusion. The following indicators draw on data from this source:

- **At risk of poverty:** The percentage of children living in households with an equivalised household disposable income below the 60% median.
- **Consistent poverty:** The percentage of children living in households with an equivalised household disposable income below the 60% median who experienced at least two forms of enforced deprivation.

There are two definitions of income and **'at risk of poverty'** (EU and national) used in the measures shown in this report. The key difference between the national and EU definition of income is that the national definition includes income from private pensions, while the EU definition does not. The calculation of national and EU risk of poverty measures involves the use of different equivalence scales. The purpose of an equivalence scale is to account for the size and composition of different income units (households) and thus allows for a more accurate comparison between households.

The national equivalence scale used to obtain the equivalised household size attributes a weight of 1.0 to the first adult in a household, 0.66 to each subsequent adult (aged 14+ living in the household) and 0.33 to each child less than 14.

For EU at risk of poverty rates, the equivalised disposable income for each person is calculated as the total net income figure divided by the equivalised household size according to the modified OECD scale (which gives a weight of 1.0 to the first adult, 0.5 to other persons aged 14 or over who are living in the household and 0.3 to each child aged less than 14).

In the Tables and Figures given in this report, tables with national data only use the national income definition and equivalence scale to calculate the 'risk of poverty' rate, while tables showing EU comparisons use the corresponding EU definitions.

The indicators shown in this report refer to income after social transfers are included.

In 2009, the 'at risk of poverty' threshold for an individual was €12,064.*

'Consistent poverty' is a measure designed to examine the extent to which persons at risk of poverty may be excluded and marginalised from participating in activities that are considered the norm for other people in society. To this end, a set of basic deprivation indicators (*listed below*) have been agreed. Persons in consistent poverty are defined as persons who are at risk of poverty (national measure) and who live in households deprived, through inability to afford them, of two or more of the following basic deprivation items:

- Two pairs of strong shoes.
- A warm waterproof overcoat.
- Buy new (not second-hand) clothes.
- Eat a meal with meat, chicken, fish (or vegetarian equivalent) every second day.
- Have a roast joint or its equivalent once a week.
- Had to go without heating during the last year through lack of money.
- Keep the home adequately warm.

* Central Statistics Office (2010) *Survey on Income and Living Conditions: 2009*. Dublin: Government Publications.

- Buy presents for family or friends at least once a year.
- Replace any worn-out furniture.
- Have family or friends for a drink or meal once a month.
- Have a morning, afternoon or evening out in the last fortnight for entertainment.

Health Behaviour of School-aged Children (HBSC) Survey: Health Promotion Research Centre

The Health Behaviour in School-aged Children (HBSC) Survey is conducted in Ireland by the Health Promotion Research Centre on a quadrennial basis. This comprises self-report, self-completion questionnaires completed by children in schools. The following indicators draw on data from this source:

- Percentage of children who report that they find it easy to talk to their mother when something is really bothering them.
- Percentage of children who report that they find it easy to talk to their father when something is really bothering them.
- Percentage of children who report to have 3 or more friends of the same gender.
- Percentage of children who report having a pet of their own or a pet in their family.
- Percentage of children who report to have been bullied in school (in the past couple of months).
- Percentage of children who report that students at their school participate in making the school rules.
- Percentage of children who report smoking cigarettes every day.
- Percentage of children who report to have been drunk at least once in the last 30 days.
- Percentage of children who report having taken cannabis at least once in their lifetime.
- Percentage of children who report feeling happy with the way they are.
- Percentage of children who report being happy with their lives at present.
- Percentage of children who report to be physically active for at least 60 minutes per day on more than 4 days per week.
- Percentage of children who report to eat breakfast 5 or more days per week.
- Percentage of children who report feeling safe in the area where they live.
- Percentage of children who report that there are good places in their area to spend their free time.

Data are subject to potential bias in relation to self-presentation and memory. They may also suffer from social desirability bias.

Social class is classified into one of the following social class groups (introduced in 1996 by the CSO), which are defined on the basis of occupation:

Social Class I:	Professional
Social Class II:	Managerial
Social Class III:	Non-manual
Social Class IV:	Skilled manual
Social Class V:	Semi-skilled
Social Class VI:	Unskilled

NUTS is an acronym for the EU Nomenclature of Territorial Units for Statistics. This classification was legally established by EU Regulation No. 1059/2003 on 29 May 2003. The 8 Regional Authorities (NUTS 3 regions) were established under the Local Government Act, 1991. In Ireland, it is classified hierarchically as Level 1 – Ireland, Level 2 – Regions and Level 3 – Regional Authorities *(see Appendix 2)*.

Children are identified as Traveller children if they answered 'Yes' to the question *'Are you a member of the Traveller community?'*.

Children are identified as having a disability and/or chronic illness if they answered 'Yes' to the question *'Do you have a long-term illness, disability, or a medical condition (like diabetes, asthma, allergy or cerebral palsy) that has been diagnosed by a doctor?'*.

Children are identified as immigrants if both their parents were born outside of Ireland.

Hospital In-Patient Enquiry: Department of Health and Children

The Hospital In-Patient Enquiry (HIPE) system is an administrative data source managed by the Economic and Social Research Institute (ESRI) on behalf of the Department of Health and Children and the Health Service Executive. HIPE provides information on each hospital discharge. The following indicators draw on data from this source, which was provided by the Department of Health and Children:

- The number of hospital discharges among children.
- The number of hospital discharges among children with a diagnosis of external causes of injury or poisoning.

HIPE data for 1994-2004 were classified using ICD-9-CM. All HIPE discharges from 2005 are now coded using ICD-10-AM (the Australian Modification of ICD-10 incorporating the Australian Classification of Health Interventions). This system includes significant changes in the classification of diagnoses and procedures. This means that it is not possible to directly compare the data published for 2005-2009 in this report to previously reported data for 1994-2004.

Care must be taken not to use hospitalisation rates as a proxy for incidence or prevalence of ill-health in children. Rates are based on episodes of care such that an individual case will be counted separately in the statistics for each admission to hospital. In addition, hospital data will reflect changes in treatment protocols, as well as issues of access to care.

HIPE has covered close to 100% of the discharges from publicly funded acute hospitals in recent years.

Immunisation Uptake Statistics: Health Protection Surveillance Centre

National data on immunisation are collated by the Health Protection Surveillance Centre (HPSC) using data provided by the HSE Regions on a quarterly basis. There is no national database on immunisation. The following indicator draws on data from this source:

- The percentage uptake of the recommended doses of vaccines among children at (a) 12 months and (b) 24 months of age.

The immunisation uptake data presented relate to children who reached their first or second birthday (uptake at 12 and 24 months respectively) during the quarters/year in question and who have received the following as appropriate (i.e. depending on their age/birth cohort):

- D_3 — 3 doses of vaccine against diphtheria
- P_3 — 3 doses of vaccine against pertussis
- T_3 — 3 doses of vaccine against tetanus
- Hib_3 — 3 doses of vaccine against *Haemophilus influenzae* type b
- $Polio_3$ — 3 doses of vaccine against polio
- $HepB_3$ — 3 doses of vaccine against hepatitis B
- $MenC_3$ — 3 doses of vaccine against meningococcal group C
- $MenC_2$ — 2 doses of vaccine against meningococcal group C
- PCV_2 — 2 doses of vaccine against pneumococcal conjugate vaccine
- Hib_b — 1 booster dose of vaccine against *Haemophilus influenzae* type b after 12 months of age
- MMR_1 — 1 dose of vaccine against measles, mumps and rubella
- BCG — 1 dose of Bacillus Calmette-Guerin vaccine

Since 18 September 2006, a Hib booster was recommended at the same time as MMR_1. This followed the national Hib campaign from November 2005 to May 2006 among children less than 4 years of age. Since 1st September 2008, the new primary childhood immunisation schedule has been implemented. The changes to the primary schedule for children born on or after 1st July 2008 include:

- Introduction of a hepatitis B vaccine (as part of a 6 in 1 vaccine) given at 2, 4 and 6 months of age.
- Introduction of pneumococcal conjugate vaccine given at 2, 6 and 12 months of age.
- Change in timing of meningococcal serogroup C conjugate vaccination, now given at 4, 6 and 13 months of age.
- Change in timing of the *Haemophilus influenzae* type b vaccination, now given at 2, 4, 6 and 13 months of age.

Please see **www.immunisation.ie** for complete information on the Irish childhood immunisation schedule and changes to the schedule introduced in September 2008.

As a new childhood immunisation schedule was introduced in 2008 for those born on or after 1st July 2008, the 2009 $MenC_3$ data at 12 months are for those born between 1st January and 30th June 2008 (i.e. Quarters 1 and 2 data only) and the 2009 $HepB_3$, $MenC_2$ and PCV_2 data at 12 months are for those born between 1st July and 31st December 2008 (i.e. Quarters 3 and 4 data only).

Some of the immunisation uptake data presented in this report are incomplete. The 2008 national $MenC_3$ data **at 12 months** are incomplete as $MenC_3$ data were not available for 13 Local Health Offices (LHOs) in Quarter 3 2008. The available 2008 12-month national $MenC_3$ data may be around 98% of the national birth cohort. The 2009 data for those at 12 months are incomplete since the following were unavailable: the Quarter 1 2009 D_3, T_3, P_3 and $Polio_3$ data for 10 LHOs for those born on 31st March 2008; the Quarter 3 2009 data for 6 LHOs; the $MenC_2$ data for 13 LHOs; the PCV_2 data for 10 LHOs; and the Quarter 4 2009 data for 9 LHOs. The available 2009 national 12-month D_3, T_3, P_3, Hib_3 and $Polio_3$ cohort data may be around 88% of the 2009 national birth cohort. The $MenC_3$ cohort data are complete (for Quarters 1 and 2 2009). The available 2009 national $HepB_3$, $MenC_2$ and PCV_2 data may be around 76%, 54% and 58% respectively of (the combined Quarters 3 and 4) national birth cohorts. BCG uptake data were available for 12 LHOs from 2005 to Quarter 2 2009, and represent approximately one-third of the national birth cohort. BCG uptake data were available for 9 LHOs in Quarter 3 2009 and for 6 LHOs in Quarter 4 2009. The available 2009 national BCG cohort data may be around 27% of the national birth cohort.

The 2005 MMR_1 data **at 24 months** are incomplete since in Quarter 4 2005 MMR_1 data were not available for 10 LHOs. The 2006 MMR_1 data includes MMR_1 data for 10 LHOs, which are an estimate only (due to technical problems with extracting MMR_1 data). The 2007 Hib_b data are incomplete since data for 3 LHOs in Quarter 1 2007 and for 2 LHOs in Quarter 3 2007 were not available. The 2007 Hib_b data also include data from 4 LHOs that were an underestimate due to data extraction methods. The 2008 $MenC_3$ data are incomplete since $MenC_3$ data for 13 LHOs were not available in Quarter 3 2008. The 2008 Hib_b data are incomplete since Quarter 2 2008 data for 4 LHOs and Quarter 3 2008 for 3 LHOs were not available. The 2009 data for those at 24 months are incomplete since the following were unavailable: the Quarter 1 2009 D_3, T_3, P_3 and $Polio_3$ data for 10 LHOs for those born on 31st March 2007; the Quarter 2 2009 Hib_b uptake data for one LHO; the Quarter 4 2009 data for 3 LHOs; the Hib_b data for one LHO and Hib_b data for 4 LHOs for those given a Hib dose as part of the 5 in 1 or 6 in 1 vaccine after 12 months of age. The available 2009 national 24-month D_3, T_3, P_3, Hib_3, $Polio_3$, $MenC_3$ and MMR_1 birth cohort data may be around 98% of the national birth cohort and the available Hib_b data may be around 95% of the national birth cohort.

International data on immunisation is collated by the World Health Organization (WHO) to monitor and assess the impact of strategies and activities for reducing morbidity and mortality of vaccine-preventable diseases. In most countries, the data collected refer to the number of doses administered to the target population divided by the total estimated number of people in the target population. The target population groups vary from country to country and are dependent on the national immunisation schedule in place.

National Educational Welfare Board Database

National data on school attendance are drawn from the School Attendance Reports, which are prepared by individual schools at primary and post-primary level and collated by the National Educational Welfare Board (NEWB). The following indicator draws on data from this source:

- Percentage of children who are absent from school for 20 days or more in the school year.

For the 2007/08 school year, 95% of primary schools and 91% of post-primary schools returned School Attendance Reports to the NEWB.

Data in Table 49 present 20-day absences at the student level and data in Table 50 present 20-day absences at the school level.

National Intellectual Disability Database: Health Research Board

The National Intellectual Disability Database (NIDD) is an administrative data source managed by the Health Research Board. The NIDD was established in 1995 to provide a comprehensive and accurate information base for decision-making in relation to the planning, funding and management of services for people with an intellectual disability. The following indicator draws on data from this source:

- The number of children under 18 years registered as having an intellectual disability.

Currently, there is approximately 95% coverage on the NIDD. Participation in this database is voluntary and only includes those in receipt of, or requiring, specialised disability services; therefore, the NIDD may not include all people living in Ireland who have an intellectual disability.

National Perinatal Reporting System: Economic and Social Research Institute

The National Perinatal Reporting System (NPRS) is an administrative data source managed by the Economic and Social Research Institute (ESRI) on behalf of the Department of Health and Children and the Health Service Executive. The NPRS provides details of national statistics on perinatal events (live births, late foetal deaths and still births). The information collected includes data on pregnancy outcomes, with particular reference to perinatal mortality and important aspects of perinatal care. In addition, descriptive social and biological characteristics of mothers giving birth and their babies are recorded. The following indicators draw on data from this source:

- Percentage of babies born weighing less than 2,500 grams (live and still births).
- Percentage of infants who are breastfed (exclusive or combined) on discharge from hospital.
- Percentage of mothers attending for antenatal care in the first trimester of pregnancy.

The collection of data on timing of first antenatal contact variable attempts to capture important information on Irish women's first contact with the healthcare services during pregnancy. This variable acts as an indicator of the length of antenatal care each mother has received and can be examined with birth, still birth and mortality rates. The completion of this indicator at present, however, may not provide an accurate estimation of this information. Although 79.1% of total births were recorded as receiving combined antenatal care in 2008, the date of the first visit to the doctor was recorded as 'not known' for 43.4% of these births. As a result of the absence of these data, the timing of first contact with health professionals within this category will reflect the date of the first hospital visit, even though this is likely to have been later than the first doctor visit.

National Physical and Sensory Disability Database: Health Research Board

The National Physical and Sensory Disability Database (NPSDD) is an administrative data source managed by the Health Research Board. The NPSDD was established in 2000 to provide a comprehensive and accurate information base for decision-making in relation to the planning, funding and management of services for people with a physical and/or sensory disability. The following indicator draws on data from the NPSDD:

- The number of children under 18 years registered as having a physical and/or sensory disability.

Currently, there is approximately 65% coverage on the NPSDD. Participation in this database is voluntary and only includes those in receipt of, or requiring, specialised disability services who are aged under 66 years of age; therefore, the NPSDD may not include all people living in Ireland who have a physical and/or sensory disability.

National Psychiatric In-Patient Reporting System: Health Research Board

The National Psychiatric In-Patient Reporting System (NPIRS) is an administrative data source managed by the Health Research Board. The data collected for the NPIRS include demographic data relating to each patient (such as gender, date of birth, marital status, address from which admitted and socio-economic group), together with clinical and diagnostic information (such as date of admission/discharge, legal category, order of admission, diagnosis on admission and discharge in accordance with the WHO International Classification of Diseases categories (ICD 10), and reason for discharge). The following indicator draws on data from the NPIRS:

- Number and percentage of admissions to psychiatric hospitals among children.

Patient Treatment Register: National Treatment Purchase Fund

The Patient Treatment Register (PTR) is an administrative data source managed by the National Treatment Purchase Fund. This on-line register of patients on in-patient and day-case surgical and medical waiting lists in Ireland has been operational since September 2005 and now includes information from 44 hospitals *(see below)*. The following indicator draws on data from the PTR:

- Number of children on hospital waiting lists (surgical and medical).

Bantry General Hospital
Beaumont Hospital, Dublin
Cappagh Orthopaedic Hospital
Cavan General Hospital**
Children's University Hospital, Temple Street**
Connolly Hospital, Blanchardstown
Cork University Hospital
Kerry General Hospital
Letterkenny General Hospital
Lourdes Orthopaedic Hospital, Kilcreene**
Louth County Hospital**
Mallow General Hospital
Mater Hospital, Dublin
Mayo General Hospital
Mercy University Hospital, Cork
Merlin Park Hospital, Galway
Midlands Regional Hospital, Mullingar
Midlands Regional Hospital, Portlaoise
Midlands Regional Hospital, Tullamore
Mid-Western Regional Hospital, Croom
Mid-Western Regional Hospital, Dooradoyle
Mid-Western Regional Hospital, Ennis
Mid-Western Regional Hospital, Nenagh
Monaghan General Hospital**
Naas General Hospital
Our Lady of Lourdes Hospital, Drogheda**
Our Lady's Hospital for Sick Children, Crumlin
Our Lady's Hospital, Navan**
Portiuncula Hospital
Roscommon County Hospital
Royal Victoria Eye and Ear Hospital, Dublin
Sligo General Hospital
South Infirmary – Victoria Hospital, Cork
South Tipperary General Hospital**
St. Colmcille's Hospital, Loughlinstown
St. James's Hospital, Dublin
St. John's Hospital, Limerick*
St. Luke's Hospital, Kilkenny**
St. Michael's Hospital, Dun Laoghaire
St. Vincent's University Hospital, Dublin
Tallaght Hospital (AMNCH), Dublin
University College Hospital, Galway
Waterford Regional Hospital**
Wexford General Hospital**

* St. John's Hospital has been unable to provide information in prescribed extract format since May 2009.

** These hospitals have not returned data since January due to industrial action. Waiting list volumes for these hospitals are the most recent data received.

The PTR only includes children who have been assessed at an out-patient clinic as in need of a surgical or medical procedure; it does not include children who are waiting to be seen at an out-patient clinic.

Programme of International Student Assessment (PISA) Survey: Education Research Centre

The Programme of International Student Assessment (PISA) Survey is conducted in Ireland by the Education Research Centre on a triennial basis. This comprises self-report, self-completion questionnaires completed by children in schools. The following indicators draw on data from this source:

- Percentage of children aged 15 who report that their parents spend time just talking with them several times a week.
- Percentage of children aged 15 who report that their parents discuss with them how well they are doing at school more than once a week.
- Percentage of children aged 15 who report that their parents eat a main meal with them around a table more than once a week.
- Percentage of children aged 15 who report that reading is one of their favourite hobbies.

These data may be subject to bias in relation to self-presentation and memory. They may suffer from social desirability bias.

PISA also includes an assessment of 'literacy'. In 2009, reading was a major assessment domain in PISA, meaning that it was comprehensively assessed, using a large number of test items. Mathematical literacy and science literacy were minor assessment domains. The following indicators draw on data from this source:

- Mean score for children aged 15 based on OECD-PISA Reading Literacy Scale.
- Mean score for children aged 15 based on OECD-PISA Mathematics Literacy Scale.
- Mean score for children aged 15 based on OECD-PISA Combined Scientific Literacy Scale.

The figures referred to as the OECD 'mean score' refer to the OECD 'country average', i.e. it is the average of the country means and not of all the OECD students pooled together.

Children are identified as Traveller children if they answer 'Yes' to the question '*Are you a member of the Traveller community?*'. In 2009, 2% of 15-year-olds in PISA reported that they were members of the Traveller community.

Children are identified as immigrants if the answer is not 'Republic of Ireland' to the question '*In what country were you and your parents born?*'. The percentage of immigrant children in PISA increased from 2.3% in 2000 to 8.3% in 2009. Some immigrant children in Ireland speak English or Irish as their first language.

Triennial Assessment of Housing Needs: Department of the Environment, Heritage and Local Government

The Triennial Assessment of Housing Needs is conducted by the Department of the Environment, Heritage and Local Government on a triennial basis. The following indicator draws on data from this source:

- Number of households with children identified as being in need of social housing.

Data represent net need for social housing, meaning households who have been assessed as being in need of either Local Authority or voluntary housing. The terminology used to describe a Local Authority's housing needs varies. These figures are net of duplicate applications (i.e. applicants who have applied to more than one Local Authority). A Local Authority's waiting list may contain duplicate applications.

One of the weaknesses of Local Authority Assessments of Housing Needs (LAAHNs) is that they do not measure severity of housing need and all households on housing waiting lists are treated as though they have an equal level of housing need. This means that there may be some people registered on housing waiting lists who have a very low housing need. On the other hand, LAAHNs may underestimate other elements of housing need. For example, Local Authorities are asked to exclude from the final figure certain households that are not assessed as suitable for Local Authority housing, namely:

- Households whose need for assistance could, in the opinion of the Authority, be more appropriately met by rent or mortgage supplementation under the Supplementary Welfare Allowance Scheme. Arguably, this highly unsatisfactory category was originally a euphemism for single people, who were not seen as appropriate for housing by Local Authorities.
- Households living in unfit Local Authority housing.
- Households living in overcrowded or materially unsuitable Local Authority housing.
- Households whose need could be more appropriately met by other social housing measures (this includes households with a particular need in addition to their housing need).

Vital Statistics: Central Statistics Office

Vital statistics relating to births, deaths and marriages are compiled by the Central Statistics Office on an annual basis. The following indicators draw on data from this source:

- Number of deaths of children under 18.
- Number of births to mothers aged 10-17.
- Number of suicides of children aged 10-17.

Deaths are coded according to the 9th Revision of the International Statistical Classification of Diseases, Injuries and Causes of Death. Stillborn babies are excluded from infant mortality figures, which refer to deaths of children aged less than one year. The mortality figures refer to crude death rates and are classified by year of registration.

Births to mothers aged 10-17 years include a small number of births to mothers aged 10-14 years. The denominator used to calculate the birth rate of mothers aged 10-17 is based on the population age group 15-17 years (rather than 10-17 years). Births relate to registered live births and exclude stillborn babies.

Suicides of children aged 10-17 years include a small number of suicides of children aged 10-14 years. The denominator used to calculate the suicide rate of children aged 10-17 is based on the population age group 15-17 years (rather than 10-17 years).

WHO European Childhood Obesity Surveillance Initiative: National Nutrition Surveillance Centre

The WHO European Childhood Obesity Surveillance Initiative is conducted in Ireland by the National Nutrition Surveillance Centre. This collects the weight, height and waist circumference of primary school children aged 7.0 - 7.9 years. The following indicator draws on data from this source:

- The percentage of children aged 7 in BMI categories: normal, overweight and obese.

The measurements were recorded over the period 10 April – 26 June 2008. Height was recorded to the last 0.1cm, weight recorded to the last 0.1kg and waist circumference to the last mm. Training in standardised measurement techniques and standard equipment was provided to 30 nutritionists who carried out the fieldwork.

APPENDIX 2: NUTS CLASSIFICATIONS

NUTS is an acronym for the EU Nomenclature of Territorial Units for Statistics. This classification was legally established by EU Regulation No. 1059/2003 on 29 May 2003. The 8 Regional Authorities for Ireland (NUTS 3 Regions), which were established under the Local Government Act, 1991, are set out below:

NUTS 2 Regions	Regional Authorities (NUTS 3 Regions)	Constituent counties (NUTS 4 Regions)	Type of area
Border, Midland and Western	**Border**	Cavan	Administrative county
		Donegal	Administrative county
		Leitrim	Administrative county
		Louth	Administrative county
		Monaghan	Administrative county
		Sligo	Administrative county
	Midlands	Laois	Administrative county
		Longford	Administrative county
		Offaly	Administrative county
		Westmeath	Administrative county
	West	Galway	County Borough
		Galway	Administrative county
		Mayo	Administrative county
		Roscommon	Administrative county
Southern and Eastern	**Dublin**	Dublin	County Borough
		Dun Laoghaire/Rathdown	Administrative county
		Fingal	Administrative county
		South Dublin	Administrative county
	Mid-East	Kildare	Administrative county
		Meath	Administrative county
		Wicklow	Administrative county
	Mid-West	Clare	Administrative county
		Limerick	County Borough
		Limerick	Administrative county
		Tipperary North Riding	Administrative county

continued

NUTS 2 Regions	Regional Authorities (NUTS 3 Regions)	Constituent counties (NUTS 4 Regions)	Type of area
Southern and Eastern *(continued)*	**South-East**	Carlow Kilkenny Tipperary South Riding Waterford Waterford Wexford	Administrative county Administrative county Administrative county County Borough Administrative county Administrative county
	South-West	Cork Cork Kerry	County Borough Administrative county Administrative county

INDEX

A

absenteeism from school, 70-72, 212
accidents and injuries, 96-99
alcohol use, 126-29
antenatal care
  attendance in first trimester of pregnancy, 179-81
  National Perinatal Reporting System (NPRS), 213
asylum, separated children seeking, 34, 201
Australian Classification of Health Interventions (ICD-10-AM), 209

B

birth rate among girls aged 10-17, 134-36, 218
birth weight, 86-88, 213
body mass index (BMI) weight categories, 100, 218
breakfast, eating, 149-52
breastfeeding, 89-92, 213
bullying among children, 57-60

C

cannabis use. *See* smoking cannabis
capitation criteria for early childhood care and education (ECCE) services, 68-69, 205-6
care, children and young people in, 191-94, 201
Census of Population
  definitions of indicators, 200-1
Central Statistics Office, 200, 202, 206, 217-18
'child', definition of (Census of Population), 200
child welfare and protection
  Childcare Interim Dataset, 201-2
  confirmed child abuse cases, 112-14, 201
  initial assessments of concerns, 109-11, 201
  types of abuse, 112
  types of concerns, 109
Child Well-Being Indicators, National Set of, 2
  definitions of indicators, 200-218
  disaggregation of data, 4
  new indicators (2010), 3
  statistical significance testing, 4
  updating indicator data, 3
Childcare Interim Dataset, 201-2
Childcare Module, Quarterly National Household Survey, 202-3
childcare, non-parental
  definition of 'childcare' (CSO), 203
  ECCE Database, 205-6
  enrolment in, 64-65
  Free Pre-School Year (ECCE) Scheme, 68-69, 205-6
  parental satisfaction with, 66-67
  quality of, 68-69
  types of childcare, 202
chronic illness. *See* disability
City and County Childcare Committees, 206
community characteristics
  children feeling safe in area where they live, 165-68
  good places in area to spend free time, 169-73
country comparisons. *See* individual indicators
county comparisons. *See* individual indicators
CSO. *See* Central Statistics Office

D

data sources, 2-3, 200-218
death rate. *See* mortality
decision-making, participation of children in, 116-19
Delivering Equality of Opportunity in Schools (DEIS), 70-71
Department of Education and Skills, 203
Department of Health and Children
  Hospital In-Patient Enquiry (HIPE), 209-10
  National Perinatal Reporting System (NPRS), 213
Department of the Environment, Heritage and Local Government, 217
deprivation indicators of consistent poverty, 160, 207-8
disability
  children with a, 32-33
  definition of (Census of Population), 201
  intellectual disability, 101-4, 213
  National Intellectual Disability Database (NIDD), 213
  National Physical and Sensory Disability Database (NPSDD), 214
  physical and/or sensory disability, 105-8, 214
  See also individual indicators
disaggregation of data, 4
drinking. *See* alcohol use
drug use. *See* smoking cannabis

E

early childhood care and education
- capitation criteria for ECCE services, 68-69, 205-6
- ECCE Database, 205-6
- enrolment in, 64-65
- Free Pre-School Year (ECCE) Scheme, 68-69, 205-6
- parental satisfaction with, 66-67
- quality of, 68-69

Early Childhood Care and Education (ECCE) Database, 205-6
eating habits. *See* breakfast, eating
ECCE. *See* early childhood care and education
Economic and Social Research Institute (ESRI), 209, 213
education
- definition of 'parental education level' (Census of Population), 200-1
- literacy/numeracy levels, 75-83
- parental education level, 22-25
- public expenditure on education, 154-57, 203-5
- school attendance, 70-72
- transfer to second level, 73-74

Education Research Centre, 216
environment
- children feeling safe in local area, 165-68
- recreation places in local area, 169-73

equivalence scale (household), 207
EU-27 Member States, comparisons with. *See* individual indicators
EU-SILC. *See* Survey on Income and Living Conditions, EU
exercise. *See* physical activity

F

family
- childcare arrangements, 64-67
- children's relationships
  - with parents, 35-60
- eating meals together, 48-49
- foster homes, 191
- lone-parent households, 19-21
- structure of, 19-21
- talking together, 44-45

father and child relationship, 40-43
foreign national children
- definition of (Census of Population), 201
- population in Ireland, 28-31
- *See also* individual indicators

foster family homes, 191
Free Pre-School Year (ECCE) Scheme, 68-69, 205-6
friendships among children, 50-53

G

Garda Juvenile Diversion Programme
- referrals to, 174-78
- Report of the Committee Appointed to Monitor the Effectiveness of the Diversion Programme, 200

Gross Domestic Product (GDP), 154, 204
Gross National Income (GNI), 154, 204

H

happiness, self-reported, 140-42
HBSC surveys. *See* Health Behaviour in School-aged Children Survey
health
- accessibility of services for children, 189-90
- alcohol use, 126-29
- antenatal care, 179-81, 213
- birth weight, 86-88, 213
- breastfeeding, 89-92, 213
- child welfare and protection, 109-14
- children on waiting lists, 189-90, 214-15
- disability, 32-33, 101-8
- hospitalisation of children, 93-99
- immunisation uptake rates, 182-88, 210-12
- mental health, 195-97, 214
- overweight and obese children, 100, 218
- sexual health and behaviour, 134-36
- smoking cannabis, 130-33
- smoking cigarettes, 122-25
- *See also* hospitalisation of children

Health Behaviour in School-aged Children (HBSC) Survey
- indicators in, 208-9

Health Promotion Research Centre, 208
Health Protection Surveillance Centre (HPSC), 210
Health Research Board, 213, 214

Health Service Executive (HSE)
child welfare and protection, 109-14, 201-2
Childcare Interim Dataset, 201-2
children and young people in care, 191-94, 201-2
Health Protection Surveillance Centre (HPSC), 210
Hospital In-Patient Enquiry (HIPE), 209-10
Local Health Offices and immunisation uptake data, 211-12
National Perinatal Reporting System (NPRS), 213
health services, accessibility for children, 189-90
hobbies. *See* reading as a leisure activity
Hospital In-Patient Enquiry (HIPE), 209-10
hospitalisation of children
accidents and injuries, 96-99
discharges from hospital, 93-99, 209-10
principal diagnosis (main causes), 93-94
psychiatric hospital admissions, 195-97, 214
waiting lists for children, 189-90, 214-15
hospitals on Patient Treatment Register (PTR), 189-90, 214-15
housing, social
households with children in need, 162-64
Local Authority Assessments of Housing Needs (LAAHNs), 217
Triennial Assessment of Housing Needs, 217
HSE Regions comparisons. *See* individual indicators

I

immigrant children
definition of (HBSC), 209
definition of (PISA), 216
See also individual indicators
immunisation for children
childhood immunisation schedule (2008), 211
uptake rates at 12 and 24 months, 182-88, 210-12
indicators of children's well-being. *See* Child Well-Being Indicators, National Set of
intellectual disability, 101-4, 213
International Classification of Diseases
ICD-10-AM, 209
ICD-9-CM, 209
international comparisons. *See* individual indicators
International Statistical Classification of Diseases, Injuries and Causes of Death, 9th Revision of, 218

K

key findings of 2010 *State of the Nation's Children* report, 4-8

L

leisure activity. *See* reading; physical activity
literacy
in mathematics, 78-80, 216
in reading, 75-77, 216
in science, 81-84, 216
Local Authority Assessments of Housing Needs (LAAHNs), exclusion criteria of, 217
Local Authority housing. *See* housing, social
Local Health Offices (LHOs)
provision of immunisation uptake data for children, 211-12
lone-parent households. *See* family

M

mathematics, children's literacy in, 78-80, 216
mental health
National Psychiatric In-Patient Reporting System (NPIRS), 214
psychiatric hospital admissions, 195-97
reasons for admissions, 195-96
See also happiness; self-esteem; suicide among youth
mortality
among children, 14-18
among infants (under 1 year), 14, 15, 16-17, 218
causes of death, 15-16
mother and child relationship, 36-39

N

National Data and Research Strategy on Children's Lives, iii
National Educational Welfare Board (NEWB) Database, 212
National Framework of Qualifications of Ireland (NFQ), 205
National Intellectual Disability Database (NIDD), 213
National Nutrition Surveillance Centre, 218
National Perinatal Reporting System (NPRS), 213

National Physical and Sensory Disability Database (NPSDD), 214
National Psychiatric In-Patient Reporting System (NPIRS), 214
National Treatment Purchase Fund, 214
Nomenclature of Territorial Units for Statistics, EU. *See* NUTS classifications
NUTS classifications, 209, 219-20
NUTS Regions comparisons. *See* individual indicators

O

obese children, 100, 218
Obesity Taskforce Standards, International, 100
OECD-PISA Literacy Scales
    combined scientific, 81-84, 216
    mathematics, 78-80, 216
    reading, 75-77, 216
offences by youth, types of, 174-76
Office of the Minister for Children and Youth Affairs (OMCYA), 4, 205
OMCYA. *See* Office of the Minister for Children and Youth Affairs
outcomes for children
    data sources, 2
    education, 63-83
    health, 85-114
    nutritional, 100, 149-52
    social, emotional and behavioural, 115-52
overweight children, 100, 218

P

parents
    children's relationships with, 36-49
    definition of 'parental education level' (Census of Population), 200-1
    early childhood care and education, 64-69
    eating meals with their children, 48-49
    education level of mothers, 22-25, 200-1
    involvement in children's schooling, 46-47
    lone-parent families, 19-21
    relationship with fathers, 40-43
    relationship with mothers, 36-39
    satisfaction with early childhood care and education, 66-67
    talking with their children, 44-45
participation of children in school decision-making, 116-19
Patient Treatment Register (PTR), 214-15
peers, children's relationships with, 50-53, 57-60
pets and animals in family, 54-56
physical activity, time spent in, 145-48
physical disability, 105-8, 214
PISA surveys. *See* Programme of International Student Assessment Survey
Population Estimates (CSO), 200
population of children
    children with a disability, 32-33
    foreign national children, 28-31
    separated children seeking asylum, 34
    total in Ireland, 10-13
    Traveller community, 26-27
poverty
    at risk of poverty, 158-59, 206-7
    consistent poverty, 160-61, 207-8
    definition of 'income', 207
    deprivation indicators, 160, 207-8
pregnancy
    antenatal care during trimesters, 179-81, 213
Programme of International Student Assessment (PISA) Survey
    assessment domains in, 76, 79, 82, 216
    indicators in, 216
psychiatric hospital admissions among children, 195-97, 214
public expenditure on education
    Ireland and EU-27, 154-57, 203-5

Q

Quarterly National Household Survey, 202

R

reading
    as a leisure activity, 120-21
    children's literacy in, 75-77, 216
relationships, children's
    data sources, 2
    with parents and peers, 35-60

S

School Support Programme (SSP), 70
schools
  attendance at, 70-72, 212
  bullying in, 57-60
  DEIS schools, 70-71
  Free Pre-School Year (ECCE) Scheme, 68-69, 205-6
  national, 73
  parental involvement in children's schooling, 46-47
  participation of students in decision-making, 116-19
  'pre-school', definition of (CSO), 203
  'primary school', definition of (CSO), 203
  School Attendance Reports, 212
  transfer to second-level education, 73-74
science, children's literacy in, 81-84, 216
self-esteem, 137-39
sensory disability, 105-8, 214
sexual health and behaviour, 134-36
smoking
  cannabis, 130-33
  cigarettes, 122-25
social class groups, definition of (CSO), 209
socio-demographics of children in Ireland, 9-34
  data sources, 2, 200-1, 217-18
statistical significance testing, 4
stillborn babies, 86-88, 213, 218
suicide among youth, 143-44, 218
supports for children
  data sources, 2-3
  formal and informal, 153-98
Survey on Income and Living Conditions, EU (EU-SILC), 206-8

T

teenage pregnancy, 134-36, 218
Traveller community
  children in, 26-27
  definition of 'Traveller' (Census of Population), 201
  See also individual indicators
Triennial Assessment of Housing Needs, 217

V

vaccination. *See* immunisation for children
Vital Statistics (CSO), 217-18

W

waiting lists
  for hospitalisation of children, 189-90
  for Local Authority social housing, 217
  hospitals on Patient Treatment Register (PTR), 214-15
World Health Organization (WHO)
  collation of international data on immunisation, 212
  European Childhood Obesity Surveillance Initiative, 218
  International Classification of Diseases (ICD-10), 209, 214

NOTES

NOTES